P9-EDM-284

SMASH THE PYRAMID

SMASH THE PYRAMID

100 CAREER SECRETS FROM AMERICA'S FASTEST-RISING EXECUTIVES

William Doyle & William Perkins

WARNER BOOKS

A Time Warner Company

Copyright © 1994 by William Doyle and William Perkins
All rights reserved.

Warner Books, Inc., 1271 Avenue of the Americas, New York, NY 10020

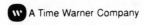 A Time Warner Company

Printed in the United States of America

First Printing: August 1994

10 9 8 7 6 5 4 3 2 1

Library of Congress Cataloging-in-Publication Data

Doyle, William, 1957–
    Smash the pyramid : 100 career secrets from America's fastest
rising executives / William Doyle and William Perkins.
        p.   cm.
    ISBN 0-446-51760-7
    1. Executives—United States—Attitudes.   2. Executive ability.
I. Perkins, William, 1953–   II. Title.
HD38.25.U6D68   1994
658.4—dc20   93-41819
                                                                  CIP

Book design by H. Roberts

To our families:
William, Sr., Marilou and Kate Doyle,
Edwin Grant, Sr., Lillian, and Edwin Grant, Jr.

CONTENTS

The Journey

You're about to take a journey into the hearts and minds of some of the fastest-rising and most successful executives in American business.

You'll travel from the polished marble halls of one of Wall Street's most powerful investment banks, to the organized chaos of one of advertising's fastest-growing agencies, to the corridors of a multinational consumer packaged-goods giant.

You'll meet top executives in finance, marketing, operations, research, legal, sales, planning, and general management, at firms ranging from America's hottest small companies to the Fortune 500.

They've worked for companies like Apple, Disney, General Electric, McKinsey, Marriott, IBM, CBS, First Boston, and Merrill Lynch, to name a few (to assure anonymity, none of these are current affiliations), as well as a variety of smaller and newer businesses.

In the pages that follow, the fastest-rising executives in America are going to shut the door, cut through the bull, candidly describe their triumphs, screwups, and failures, and reveal to you 100 major "secrets" they've uncovered for succeeding in a business career.

In blunt, occasionally colorful language, the "superstars" of business are going to explain how careers really work.

There are plenty of good books on the market about management theory, paradigms, excellence, quality control, and entrepreneurship.

This isn't one of them.

Instead, this book is designed exclusively *to give you 100 distinct competitive career advantages* to help you protect your job, improve your performance, and prosper in today's chaotic and sometimes brutal business environment.

The Mystery of the Pyramid

Several years ago we worked together at the J. Walter Thompson advertising agency in New York. One day we sat down for lunch in the company cafeteria and began watching the procession of executives in their twenties, thirties, and early forties bantering their way through the chow line.

Some of them were racing quickly up the organizational "pyramid" to claim positions with huge salaries and major operating responsibilities.

A great many others were getting stuck in the middle to lower ranks, thanks to the enormous number of "baby boom" and "Generation X" managers competing for careers and promotions in an era when this and many other American companies were slashing their workforces.

Suddenly it hit us. *We had almost no idea why some were rising quickly and others weren't.*

To be sure, a few were "rocket scientists" and others were just plain lucky. But most of the rest seemed equally smart and hardworking.

We speculated that one thing that separated many of the "fast risers" must be that **they were simply more quickly figuring out which patterns of attitudes and behavior succeed in today's business environment and which don't.**

We then wondered whether there might be an invisible, or "secret," body of knowledge available in the collective experiences of such executives that could help us in our own careers.

We looked around, but we couldn't find it.

While the bookstores were brimming with business success titles, they all seemed to be about entrepreneurs or elder statesmen/CEOs whose experiences were either several decades or several billion dollars removed from our own, or written by people whose career experience was limited to companies we'd never heard of.

None examined the experiences of what seemed to us to be the most interesting source—the men and women in their twenties, thirties, and early forties who weren't yet CEOs but were rising quickly up the corporate ladder to become senior vice presidents, CFOs, executive vice presidents, and division and company presidents early in their careers. So we decided to try to pull it together ourselves.

Unlocking the Secrets of the Pyramids

Right now the pyramids of business are being smashed and flattened by accelerating global competition, technology shifts, and corporate restructuring. There's never been a more urgent time for challenging conventional career wisdom and reexamining traditional assumptions about "how to succeed."

To that end, we sat down with sixty of the fastest-rising executives across America in a series of in-depth, one-on-one interviews and persuaded them to reveal the strategies they've discovered for achieving career success and avoiding career disaster.

Our criteria for selecting the executives was simple: They must have reached a senior position at their company (for example, the senior vice president level or the equivalent in their industry or company), before the age of forty.

The executives were identified primarily through a three-year search of company articles, career reportage, and executive appointments and promotions columns of business publications like the *Wall Street Journal, Fortune, Forbes,* and *BusinessWeek,* plus specialized publications such as *Advertising Age, Variety, Black Enterprise,* and *Working Woman.*

The panel includes executives from companies in the *Fortune* 500, *Fortune's* 100 Fastest-Growing Companies, and *BusinessWeek's* Best Small Companies reports, among others.

Executives were invited to participate by letter and were sent a discussion guide prior to the interviews. Each panelist was offered an honorarium to be paid to their designated charity.

We guaranteed each panelist that *their remarks would be anonymous*—encouraging them to open up and speak in total candor. We felt this was essential because we wanted a completely uncensored, uninhibited, and freewheeling discussion, including any "dirt" they've observed in their race up the corporate ladder.

We asked our subjects to skip the "warm and fuzzies" and to concentrate on the harsh realities and behind-the-scenes struggles of a business career; to describe the land mines they wish they hadn't sat down on, the most irrational bosses they've had to manage, their best days in business, and their worst screwups and biggest surprises; and to reveal the "secrets" they wish they had known about years ago.

Who They Are

We conducted *in-depth interviews with sixty executives.* More than two-thirds of them are quoted in the book.

Some have Ivy League degrees and MBAs. Many do not. In fact, several skipped college entirely.

We strove to select executives from a balanced mix of large, medium, and small companies.

The executives represent a broad cross-section of industries, from high-tech manufacturing and computer software to global mining and mineral exploration, motion picture production, investment banking, advertising, media, corporate law, health care, consumer packaged goods, telecommunications, fashion, retail, automobile manufacturing, publishing, management consulting, and many others.

Almost half of the executives are women.

Approximately *25 percent are ethnic minorities,* including African-, Hispanic-, and Asian-Americans.

All but two were forty years old or younger at the time of the interviews. The oldest executive was forty-three, the youngest twenty-nine. The average age was thirty-seven.

Interviews were conducted with executives in forty cities around the country, in seventeen states: New York, California, Illinois, Florida, Texas, Maryland, Georgia, Louisiana, Arizona, Nevada, Pennsylvania, New Jersey, Massachusetts, Michigan, Missouri, Iowa, Colorado, and Washington, D.C.

The 100 Secrets

Our goal in doing the interviews was not to produce a scientific treatise, but to uncover a "menu" of uncensored insights, anecdotes, and lessons learned that you can apply, as appropriate, to your career.

While our panelists represent a wide range of corporate cultures and management experiences, we were struck by how often themes kept repeating through the interviews and by how frequently insights connected to one another across industries.

Some of the secrets are new "spins" on familiar themes.

Others describe realities of interpersonal and organizational behavior that we've rarely seen covered in the management textbooks and business press, and that we wish someone had told us about years ago.

Some secrets describe things to do; others reveal "minefields" of behavior you should avoid at all costs.

We divided the secrets into three groups—Managing Yourself, Managing People, and Managing the Work.

The names and summaries of the secrets are ours, and are intended as a road map through the insights of the panelists.

All the quotes are from the executives themselves. We wanted to deliver them to you as directly as possible, without bias or reinterpretation. Some feature strong language, which we chose to include, since this is the way people often actually speak.

We hope that by exposing you to the mistakes, triumphs,

and uncensored comments of a remarkable group of fellow managers, this journey will give you new perspectives and equip you with a portfolio of insights that will help your career flourish more quickly.

While you're smashing your own pyramids, we also hope you manage to have some fun.

—Bill Doyle and Bill Perkins
New York City, 1994

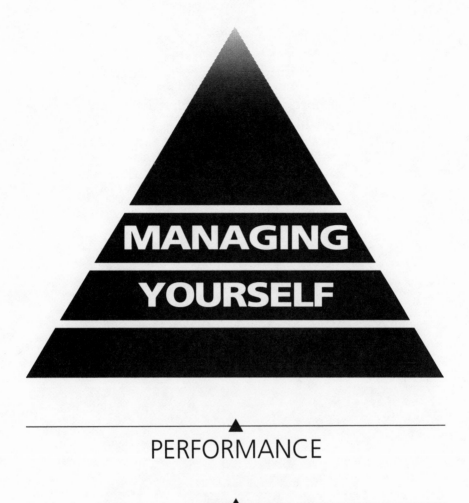

MANAGING
YOURSELF

PERFORMANCE

PERCEPTIONS

SELF-AWARENESS

The Secret of Guaranteed Injustice

A supreme reality of careers is that they are often irrational, unfair, and influenced by a multitude of subjective factors, most of them interpersonal.

▲

▲

About eighteen months into my career I realized that life isn't fair. Now that sounds like a very strange statement to make. As a black female, one would think that the last thing I should have to realize is that life isn't fair.

▲

But I had always been in an academic environment where, if you worked hard, gave it your all, and did whatever you thought was important to do, you would succeed.

Having been a bright kid, I really believed that anything you wanted and were willing to work hard for, you could get.

And then I quickly realized it wasn't about being fair.

I realized there were a lot of subjective factors that were involved in success and that I had to be a whole lot more sensitive to them. I came in and I figured, well, I'm not going to be able to be one of the chosen few, so I will wow them by my hard work.

I will just work harder and longer and smarter and better than anybody else, and God will provide.

And then came the first round of promotions to Associate Product Manager.

There were seven of us in the group and four of us were left behind. We happened to be women. It was sort of interesting.

I then sat and talked to a fellow who was in another division who had been here maybe a year and a half longer than I had. I said to him, "You seem to be doing well. Tell me why didn't I get promoted?"

He said, "Well, because it's not about the work in total. It's also about all of the other things that you do to distinguish yourself from your peers that involve interpersonal activities."

That was a hard lesson, but it was one of the first ones I learned.

It's not like anything that you've ever dealt with, because corporate life is subjective, and you've got to learn to deal with that subjectivity. Once you do that, you're fine.

I don't know that I understood that when I first came in. Or understood the importance of it. And I think it hurt me.

What I tell people now is that you've got to be able to have a strong sense of who you are, and to be comfortable projecting who you are.

I got promoted six weeks later, so it wasn't the end of the world. But those were probably the longest six weeks of my life.

▲

I think the first and foremost criteria to success is doing excellent work. You can have all the style and all the presence, and if your work stinks, you're not going to go anyplace. At the same time, if you're really good at getting the job done but there is a sense that you don't have the presence, you're not going to get anywhere.

▲

—43-year-old Division President
Consumer Packaged Goods Marketing/Manufacturing

The Secret of Productive Chaos

A little turmoil can be good for your career.

▲

▲

Organizational turmoil can really be a major source of opportunity, if looked at in the right way.

▲

A foreseeable future in Silicon Valley is approximately two years.

I've survived many waves of change and several foreseeable futures in this one company. I never really expected to be in one company that long, or to be in the position that I'm in now, which is president of the company.

I started out at the very bottom of the totem pole and ended up as the president. Part of that was because of a lot of hard work, some talent, and various other factors—factors that were within my control. But some of it was also because of a certain amount of chaos. We merged with another company, and there were several changes of top management. That gave me opportunities to move up.

With negative changes, it's easy to think, "What a disaster." But from the point of view of someone who is purposeful, linear, and high performing, those same changes are opportunities to be selected out for more responsibility.

So if the company had been totally stable, and had not gone through a lot of rock and roll and changes, I might have stayed a vice president or who knows what. I just wouldn't have had the opportunities that I had.

▲

The surprise is that chaos is not always a bad thing for any one individual.

▲

And that doesn't mean looking at it in an exploitive way. Because I never was happy during the times of turmoil. I never clapped my hands and thought, "Oh, boy, now's my chance!"

You sort of keep your group's act together under chaotic circumstances, and you keep being profitable. I was basically running the only profitable division in an unprofitable company. And I kept getting selected out for high performance.

There's a single Chinese ideogram that stands for both crisis and opportunity that is understandable in this context.

▲

Never confuse your own individual circumstances and/or performance with what happens to the company as a whole. Because your fortunes may rise or fall with the company you're with or they may rise and fall differentially.

▲

Company and individual performance are separable. And as we move into an environment where employees are seen as free agents, as opposed to wedded to a particular company, even if you stay within the same company your fortunes may be decoupled from the rise and fall of the particular situation the company is in.

They may, however, be tightly coupled to the particular team you're on.

So if you're a high-performing business unit within a poorly performing company, you can actually do very, very well. In some cases, you might do better than you would have if the whole company had been performing well.

I was in an environment where the company's overall business performance was very poor. The company was losing millions of dollars. But my business unit was consistently profitable since I started it eight years ago. It was stable while the rest of the company went through all kinds of chaos—layoffs and downsizings. I never laid off anyone in my group.

I was getting promotions and raises every year when other people either were getting laid off or getting no promotions at all.

In fact, I remember several times when all the general managers were sitting around the table and saying, "Well, you have to share the pain, because we're doing a company layoff." And I would say, "Sorry. I'm not going to do that because all of our people are billable on customer contracts, and we need them to be profitable. We're not sharing the pain under these circumstances. It would hurt the company."

▲

It's important to not just pick the company, but to pick the business unit within the company. Don't just pay attention to the performance of the overall company, but pay attention to the business unit you are joining or putting together. Because in the new environment, business units are going to be sorted by their return on investment and their profitability.

▲

The inverse is also true.

If you're with a successful company, and that successful company has nonperforming business units, and you're in one of those nonperforming business units, change it, get out, or you'll be selected out.

Procter & Gamble and GE are two recent examples of that. The overall companies are very profitable, but they lay off people or sell off nonperforming business units.

—38-year-old President
Computer Software Company

The Secret of Multidimensional Career-Pathing

Know the difference between a temporary setback and a career disaster.

▲

▲

Business careers are very much like complex chess games in that the next step is important, but it's often the three steps after that which will determine whether you win or lose. It's not always the immediate step, so you really have to be focusing a couple of leaps ahead. If you think you've become a "falling star," you should view the game plan as having multiple steps.

▲

Don't look at the next step as being a step down, but figure out whether or not two steps or three steps beyond that you will be beyond where you are currently.

You see it more in people businesses than you do in manufacturing businesses. In people businesses, somebody can become "politically out," whatever that means.

"Politically out" rarely has to do with politics; it always has to do with interpersonal chemistry—somebody just doesn't like someone.

All of a sudden everything they do is wrong. They may have been viewed as real talent, everything was positive, and all of a sudden they're out.

▲

A mistake a lot of people make is to assume that if they've fallen once, they're on a downward trend in perpetuity. That's not necessarily true. I think it's important to ride it through or at least to play it through strategically to figure out whether or not the next move beyond that could be a recovery instead.

▲

When an athlete has an injury, the athlete doesn't give up sports. But he doesn't go out the next day and try to compete in the same sport, and doesn't expect to compete as effectively as he had. Many athletes recover and exceed where they were.

On the other hand, the trap a lot of people fall into is when they are clearly on a downward spiral in an organization, each time they're notched downward, they think, "Well, this is temporary and I'll accept this, but if I stick it out and if I'm loyal and I wait, over time all of my good traits will be recognized."

The truth is that if there is a pattern of decline, or demotion, or diminution, the best advice is to make a change, and not wait for the organization to make the change for you, to make the decision for you.

▲

In other words, most people in careers suffer setbacks, and a single setback is not necessarily a sign that you're a falling star on a downward spiral.

▲

Those who don't suffer setbacks are those who have very plodding, predictable careers; they don't take chances. So chances are they move a small notch forward at a time.

But my point is that if you suffer from multiple setbacks—meaning one setback is then followed by another and possibly another—then that's the difference between a trend, a pattern, and a one-time incident.

—37-year-old Senior Managing Partner
Investment Banking Firm

The Secret of
Circuitous Ascent

Sometimes the best track to your dream
job may be an indirect one.

▲

▲

**When a promotion eludes you, you can't stew over it. You
have to get over it. It has nothing to do with fairness and
justice, because what's justice to one person isn't necessarily
justice to somebody else. Sitting there feeling like a victim
hurts you personally and professionally.**

▲

One of the biggest surprises that I had was that the job that I'm
in now is the job that, for most of my career, I was dying to have, but
it eluded me three times.

When I finally gave up on ever having it and went off in a totally
different direction, the job came my way.

You decide what college you want to go to, you decide who
you're going to marry; for many years you control the major deci-

sions in your life. And I always thought that that would be true of my career.

If I want that job, I'll just get in line, I'll work hard and do well, and I'll move up in the organization.

That works for a while, and then at some point it stops working. At some point, other things factor in.

My goal was constantly eluding me. And at one point I finally just said, all right, I've had my heart broken three times on this already, I'm going to forget it.

It's almost like getting over a relationship. However you decide to get over it, get over it.

So I ventured out on an entirely different course. Instead of running a line of business, as I had been doing, I went into strategic planning.

It was new, and I found it very interesting. I worked for somebody from whom I learned a lot and who benefited from my business experience.

Then, when the opportunity came up for what had been my elusive goal, he was my biggest supporter and biggest fan, and was very instrumental in deciding that I really was good at running a business.

Don't get distracted by thinking, "So and so got this and they didn't work any harder than me."

You can always find people who you think have gotten a better deal than you've gotten.

The lesson I learned is: Don't always think that there's only one way to achieve something, that you know the right way.

The key is that you need to be open to new experiences, to trying something else, if what you thought was going to work doesn't work.

—37-year-old Senior Vice President
Financial Institution

The Secret of Courageous Imperfection

You're probably going to screw up at least 30 percent of the time. And everybody else knows it. Have the courage to say, "I fucked up."

▲

Sometimes you think to yourself, "Oh, shit—is this the right decision? It's 50/50."

When you make decisions, you tend to get defensive about them because you know there's somebody else either openly or secretly against it, and you know they think you're an idiot.

When people make a bad decision, or there are failures of implementation with a good decision, they become rigid and are afraid to reverse themselves.

Always be prepared to reverse a bad decision.

You need to notify everyone that you're pretty sure you're going to be wrong a reasonable amount of the time, because—let's face it—you are.

▲

The people who think that they are going to politick or maneuver their way to success, or even survival, will see that that kind of behavior usually won't work. In today's environment, star quality and flashiness and charisma alone are qualities that are less admired. In the 1990s substance, integrity, and thoughtfulness are much more important.

▲

There's been a shift, even a backlash, against the "home-run hitter" who ignores teamwork, the "gamesman," the person who's only trying to create a "big idea" or a "major move."

There's more of a recognition today that business is led by sustainability.

▲

The engine of sustainability is substance, and execution, and operational know-how, and a thorough understanding of how to lead an organization, not just a single strategic move at 20,000 feet.

▲

In times of crisis, which every business has, you've got to start making hard decisions based on what's really "there."

One of my favorite stories concerns a guy who was incredibly charismatic and had been around for a long time. He knew everybody. A great backslapper.

He got up in front of his boss in an important meeting and started getting drilled.

These were simple, basic things that you'd expect him to know in order to run the business. They were things that maybe people didn't always pay attention to.

"How many engineers do you have? How many engineers per plant? Has that gone up or down? What's your productivity?"

He didn't know the answers, and was gone three months later.

The people who self-destruct sometimes are the ones who think they know they system; they understand the system, and they get success out of manipulating the system. It becomes contagious and it becomes fun. And they eventually get caught.

▲

If there's a number-one lesson, it's that a lack of integrity always catches up with you.

▲

Right now, across all businesses, if there's one thing that you can be guaranteed will get you, it is a lack of integrity.

That includes altering the results to make it look good when it's not. Spin control. Media manipulation. Putting an unrealistically good face on things. Obfuscating reality.

▲

Integrity is not just about lying, cheating, stealing. Integrity is telling people things they don't want to hear. And presenting a balanced approach in everything that's happening.

▲

—39-year-old Senior Vice President
Consumer Packaged Goods

The Secret of
Upside Volatility

The riskiest, most dangerous career situations can provide the greatest rewards.

▲

I was promoted to director of corporate accounting at a fairly stable, $1,000,000,000 company at a fairly young age.

I had a great job and it was good money, and people wondered why the hell I would risk any of that to come out here to a small, privately held company that was losing money.

I was about thirty years old and the CFO, which would have been the next position, was a forty-three-year-old guy. So there wasn't a lot that I was going to be able to do at that point.

▲

I would take the shittiest jobs that were available if they were offered to me as a promotion, in areas where other managers wouldn't go in terms of troubled staff, troubled financial con-

ditions. I figured, in my own warped way, that I can't do any worse here, and I have an opportunity to do very well. As a result of that I went into fairly risky situations, which required certainly a lot of attention, but I felt that the upside was greater.

▲

I felt that I was young enough to take a chance, and that's how I ended up here. And then I eventually started taking over more operational responsibilities.

Someone once told me that if you were going to work for a small company, you ought to go to one that was either growing wildly or in disastrous shape.

There's probably no better way to learn, much more so than in a well-established environment where there's a defined career path and a lot of executive training.

Here, executive training is on the job, and it's almost a baptism by fire in many respects. It may not be great for your digestive system, but it certainly puts enough scars on you so that you can move forward in life.

We went from losing millions of dollars every year to being profitable in a year's time to eventually taking the company public in 1991. Now we're growing at a rate of 18 to 20 percent a year. We'll be around $80 million this year.

My learning curve was accelerated dramatically, and I never thought I'd end up in a small company.

You've got to have the basic willingness to commit and learn and take chances.

We probably all ought to work for the Post Office if we think we should be risk-averse when it comes to our jobs. The likelihood of getting laid off or fired is probably high no matter where you are.

▲

There really is no job security. Companies are being forced to take pretty drastic positions in order to remain efficient and competitive. The days of retiring with some high level of compensation over the last twenty years or ten years of your career are gone.

▲

I think the issue really must be, then, why not take the risk with the opportunity to have the greatest upside as well?

Along with risk comes issues of financial solvency, market credibility, takeovers, buyouts, mergers, acquisitions—all of that stuff can end up displacing you.

There's also still the risk that you're going to fall on your face.

But the fact is that there's greater opportunity in all of those environments as well.

I don't want to sound like I took a left-handed approach to any of these things, but as long as you can define that there is opportunity in these less-than-great situations that you're being given a chance to fix, you have to look at the fact that it's already a disaster, and that all you can do is make it better.

—38-year-old President
Diagnostic Imaging Manufacturer

The Secret of
Self-Predestination

No one cares as much about your career
as you.

▲

▲

**In the end, it's up to you to manage your career. No one else
is going to manage it, okay? No matter how much they preach
about career planning and career management, and we're sitting here and we know we want to move you from this part of
the company to another part—that's bullshit.**

▲

Now for certain people, yes, there is a career plan, and those are
stars, but not everybody is a star. And everybody has to take it into
their own hands to manage their career.

If you don't take hold of your career and manage it, no one's
going to do it for you.

You've got to know when you've been working for this person
long enough, and now it's time to move on, or you've been working

for this company long enough and it's time to move on, or, "Gee, they love me here, but it would be better for me if I now started to work on something else."

You've got to be able to work that out and figure out a way to make it happen because the company probably isn't going to do it for you.

There's got to be a way, without making it a headache for your boss, to engage him in a conversation every three to six months about, "How are you feeling? How am I doing?"

I was in charge of a department of a hundred people.

Of the hundred, there were maybe a dozen that the company felt so strongly about that they were going to take the lead in managing their career. The rest were very good people, but we didn't have enough time to pay attention to planning all of their careers.

It's up to the individual, for sure.

▲

You've got to assume that the company you're working for is not going to plan your career. They may help you plan it—if you encourage it. But to assume they are going to take over and plan your career for you is just never going to happen. There is no individual in the company who has that as a priority.

▲

Some people get lucky, some people don't. But you've really got to take it into your hands.

You've got to be sitting there thinking what is the best next thing for me, and then go make it happen.

—34-year-old President
Advertising Agency

The Secret of Organizational Gratification

Overt self-promotion has become a dangerous career tactic. Tie your career instead to the basics of your business.

▲

▲

Career success in the 1990s is much more tied to the fundamentals of business rather than to self-promotion.

▲

The people who are working for themselves rather than working for the stockholders are ultimately going to get killed career-wise, when all the dust settles.

The best boss I ever had was an operating vice president in a group where I spent a few years.

What I learned from him is to always do the right things for the business. Even if it is at great political sacrifice.

He's an extremely thoughtful man. I can say categorically that every decision the man made was made in the best interest of the total corporation, even if it meant it came at a personal sacrifice or at the sacrifice of his respective operating unit. He was always working for the corporate bottom line.

He has done extremely well in terms of his career progress. He's a group executive of the company and he's only in his mid-forties, so the company has recognized him.

I enjoyed working for him the most because I knew at all times that what we were doing was trying to improve the value of this corporation to its shareholders—every decision that was made, even if it meant personal sacrifice or sacrifice by his operating division. This guy was just literally straight up. That's the way I've tried to operate.

I've never spent five minutes "managing my career." Ever. I've always dedicated every ounce that I have into doing what's right for the company.

I'm not saying that to be a company man; it's just that's why I'm here.

▲

There are other people who own the company, and if you're not operating in the best interest of the owners of the company, it's only going to be a matter of time before they're going to come asking questions.

▲

I don't care what firm you're in; I don't care how large or small it is. Management of a company is there to improve the shareholder wealth, on an ongoing basis, period.

If you're not focused on that at all times, in every decision, if you're ever "suboptimizing" that objective, either for personal reasons or for your business unit within the larger corporate entity, ultimately it's going to come back on you. And I can show you the examples.

▲

I see too many people of our generation spending a whole lot of time trying to manage their appearances rather than doing the work.

▲

What I'm making a pitch for is for people to put 110 percent into helping run their businesses to create shareholder wealth. That should be the all-consuming passion of what you're doing, rather than spending much time on self-promotion or overtly political career planning.

I'm not saying you don't have to think about what you want to get out of life—what your objectives are and how you can best meet them. But you shouldn't be spending company time on promoting yourself over the interests of the stockholders, period.

I think in the period of the 1980s, where you had high growth, or in any growth period, you had some room, some latitude to put some focus on yourself or other dimensions.

▲

But in a period like the 1990s, there's no margin for error now. There is no margin for error for any company in this economy. Customers now are all shopping value. The investors are also doing the same. You've got to produce superior value for your customers, which means you've got to really deal with the fundamentals of the business. You can't sell people fluff.

▲

I think the 1990s are going to end up being the decade of fundamentals.

Business is pretty simple. All you have to do is be able to make a product that people want and be able to produce it at a cost where you've got a margin. It's actually very simple.

I've often said that business was invented so dumb people like me can make a living.

The worst boss I ever had was somebody who spent 80 percent of their effort on self-promotion.

It isn't that the individual hasn't gotten very far; the person has.

But I still believe that ultimately the system is going to find such people out.

The real focus is on themselves, on promoting themselves. When they enter into a project, what they're really trying to do is just make themselves look more positive; whether they really produce any real value to the company is secondary. If they do, it's a happy coincidence, but it's not the focus of their effort.

Personally it was the most difficult time I ever had. It was the one time in my career when I honestly considered leaving the company.

I would come forward with recommendations and plans that were based on a different set of criteria. They were recommendations that would not necessarily be popular with senior management, so this person in the chain of command was not willing to take them forward.

I made the offer to divorce my boss from the recommendation: "I'll take it in myself and you can disavow any knowledge." Even at that level the person was not willing to let me go forward because they felt it would somehow be a negative reflection on them.

It made me feel cheap—to think that what I was doing was working to provide fodder for someone else's self-promotion.

I've seen a lot of people like this. I've since passed them in the system of things. It concerns me that they're still here. But I think they're actually slowing themselves down, and they do get found out.

—40-year-old Strategic Planning Executive
Automobile Manufacturer

The Secret of Hyperdiligent Humility

If you're pursuing a promotion or another job don't be too overt about it, and make totally sure you do the job you've got right now.

▲

When people are ambitious and rising quickly, people around them want to feed the ambition. Sometimes they feed it in what they think is a supportive way, by always talking about the next opportunity: "Are you interested in this job, in that job?"

▲

The reality is that too much ambition is a bad thing for one's career.

▲

If people end up believing that all you're interested in is the next job and you're not really committed to the current job, you won't get the next job.

And yet there are people all the time filling your head about the next job, so there's a certain amount of self-control and self-discipline involved.

You don't want to turn these people off in terms of talking about the next opportunity, assuming for the moment that their motives are good. On the other hand, whenever you're having a conversation about the next opportunity or the next level, I have found it works to keep coming back to reinforcing your commitment to do the current job as well as you can.

▲

The thing I've seen that has killed most high-flyers is not their competence, it's their lack of attention to their current assignment. They were so focused on their ambition that they forgot to do the job.

▲

Another variation on the theme is people who give the impression that they're in a job that's just a way station, an interlude.

You almost have to go into a job convinced it's the last job you're ever going to have. I've watched people go into jobs broadcasting the feeling that "in a year and a half, I'll be onto my next thing," and I think that's very self-destructive.

▲

In corporations there's this funny balance between people expecting you to be ambitious but not overly ambitious. And keeping the team play, which is an essential part of success, in balance with the desire to move ahead in business.

▲

When those things get out of balance, people get very concerned.

I have had cases where people have come to talk to me about it. There are code words for it. One is, "This is a turf issue, you're grabbing for turf." That's another way of saying, "You're acting overly ambitious here."

If you have real friends—and if you have real friends in a corporation, who you can say anything to, that number five over a lifetime, you're lucky—they'll come tell you.

Or they might tell you that you're putting on a show too often, that you're in the limelight too often.

In my current position I'm responsible for holding meetings on strategy. I realized I was stepping over the line when way too many agenda items were mine or my staff's.

No one came to see me; I just could tell people were tuning out. There was too much of me standing in front of the group. So I made an effort to get other people to bring their strategic issues before the group.

▲

A career won't succeed unless there is support from your peers as well as your subordinates.

▲

If the only thing that is happening is someone is pulling you from above in the hierarchy, it's not enough. It may be enough for the first couple of levels, but it's not enough ultimately.

It's a career killer to get too upwardly focused and to forget about your other constituents, your peers and your subordinates.

That's a nice way of saying, if you earn the reputation of being a kiss-ass, or being a son of a bitch to your support staff, it'll kill you.

▲

All of that stuff gets out in the end. I think particularly now in the '90s, if the only input on someone is that the boss thinks he's great, that's not considered complete input.

▲

To get a feeling about someone, most good bosses will always ask their peers. That feedback will either help you or kill you. If they say you're just interested in your own agenda, you're not a team player, that'll kill you, no matter who up top thinks you're great.

If your subordinates are talking about you being abusive or not being interested in the health of the organization, that will get out.

Corporate life really is a fishbowl. You can't hide a whole lot.

Those selfish "bad bosses" made it up the ladder when the culture was different.

▲

It's a reflection of American business recognizing certain realities. There's more emphasis on getting feedback from a wider set of people.

▲

It sounds corny, but I've found it to be true: Good, relevant work will get noticed.

I think it's far more important to spend your time doing the work, making sure it's truly good, truly relevant, and that it truly makes a difference. If those three things are in place, it'll get noticed.

When people think you're selling yourself instead of the work, that's a problem. If it's the work that's selling you, that's not a problem. I have never had a situation where my work didn't speak for itself.

I do think there's an overemphasis on getting ahead through self-promotion instead of getting ahead by doing work extremely well.

▲

I can think of a lot of times when I have advised subordinates, "Quit worrying about your next job; quit worrying about what people think of you; quit worrying about selling yourself and do your damn job."

▲

—37-year-old Vice President
Global Telecommunications Company

The Secret of
Theatrical
Fanaticism

Cultivate the impression that you care
passionately for the work and the
company.

▲

▲

**To clients and bosses, I try to appear as passionate, as inter-
ested, and as emotionally involved in their business as they
do. I let them know I'll lie down on the railroad track for
them. If I think an idea is good, I'm going to lie down on that
conference room table until they buy it.**

▲

Sometimes I'll even offer to pay for a project out of my own
pocket!

Once there were layoffs at a company I worked at. It was like
Sophie's Choice because my colleague and I had to choose between
two junior people, and I did not want to lose either one.

One junior person's salary was pretty small. Our solution was to
go to management and say, "Look, we will evenly divide that person's

salary and take it out of our own salaries"—that's how important it is to us.

We did this to demonstrate how strongly and deeply we felt. Obviously we wanted them to instead say, "Okay already, you can keep them!"—which they did.

When I was a junior account executive working on food products, I always let my clients know that I stopped by the supermarket after work to look around and see what's going on—who's featuring what, what new products are coming out. "Guess what I saw? There was a really interesting thing about the way your product was being featured. I thought to myself, well, perhaps x,y,z."

I always had ideas about what my clients were doing, what their competitors were doing. I tried to be the ultimate "consumer of consumers."

▲

Not many people are as passionate as that in business. When they meet someone who is, it makes a real impact.

▲

—29-year-old Senior Vice President
Communications Industry

The Secret of
Customer
Obsession

The more you understand your
customers' behavior, the faster you'll rise.

▲

I don't have a college degree.

When I started out in the retail business, I think that one of the
things that distinguished me, or at least provided me with an "equal-
izer," is the fact that I was passionately devoted to seeking out information about the consumer. I had an extremely sharp consumer focus.

I was hired as an assistant buyer at a retail chain.

I would come in to my boss and get very excited about numbers,
about consumer sales. I'd say, "Look, this color sold 10 percent more
at this store than last year. This line of dresses sold 20 percent more
in this market than in the other market."

▲

I was visibly intrigued, excited, and enthused by the effect that our business had on consumers and consumer behavior. My bosses really respected that.

▲

I became devoted to trying to understand what the consumer wants to buy and fulfilling that need.

It sounds obvious, but knowing the consumer, no matter what business you're in, is a huge asset.

—37-year-old Senior Vice President
Women's Fashion Manufacturer

The Secret of
Universal
Marketing

You may think you're in finance. Or research. Or operations. Or legal. You're wrong. We're all in sales and marketing.

▲

▲

We're all in sales and marketing. Absolutely. In everything we do.

▲

Every day, from when you sit down with somebody at lunch, to when you're sitting in your office, or talking on the phone, it's how you come across, how you present your ideas, how you present your projects, how you format your presentation.

You have to try to inject enthusiasm into everything you do—not only the overall level of enthusiasm you take to the office every day, but project by project.

If you are given something to do or you're handing off a project to somebody to do, you've got to try to inject enthusiasm into it.

As a team leader or a project leader, you're a marketer. Everybody markets something. Some people market soap, some people market gasoline.

But every day you're marketing yourself or you're marketing your project.

You're marketing your group to others to provide the services that they need and you provide. Somebody who says, "Oh, I'm not interested in sales or marketing," won't be successful working for me.

—35-year-old Senior Vice President
Global Mining and Minerals Company

The Secret of
Existential Cool

Be prepared to absorb temporary career setbacks, lateral moves, even demotions. The smoother you handle them, the more respect and currency you'll gain.

▲

▲

Sometimes not everything goes your way in your career.

▲

I started as marketing manager. I was then promoted to director of marketing. A few years later, I was promoted to vice president of marketing.

We went through a merger and a reorganization. For a period of three or four months, I had to report to a senior vice president of sales and marketing, as director of marketing.

During that period of time when my title changed downward, my gut reaction was to resign and walk away from the entire situation.

Instead I basically said to myself that this was going to be a short-term situation, and I chose to ignore it, continuing to do what I felt was the best job I could.

When I was repromoted to vice president many people came up to me and said, "I really respected you for how maturely you handled those couple of months—not many people would have done that."

One person said to me, "You needed to be bloodied up a little bit. Everything's always gone your way."

I think it made a lot of people respect me more because I handled it in such a mature fashion.

—33-year-old Senior Vice President
Health Care

The Secret of
Flexible Reality

Don't automatically accept the operating "realities" of a career situation. Today's reality may not be tomorrow's; yours may not be somebody else's.

▲

▲

People who are successful figure out that reality is influence-able, and that today's reality isn't tomorrow's. Or that their reality doesn't have to be somebody else's.

▲

My model for decision making is some of the civil rights people of the '60s.

Taking risks. Refusing to accept the status quo.

Like Rosa Parks sitting down at the front of the bus.

Or Fannie Lou Hamer, who picked cotton for forty years and then decided one day that she was going to go down and register to vote, no matter what the obstacles. That's decisiveness.

Someone did an artistic rendering of that story. I sat there and I was amazed again by the story, but then I thought about how that's part of the key to success in life, being able to make decisions and then to feel comfortable recognizing that most decisions are reversible in some way, shape, or form.

You may not like the process that reversal takes, or the time it takes or some of the implications. But it's okay.

▲

It's okay to screw it up and make another decision and go on. And you don't have to be mired down with, "Oh, why did I fail?" Screw it, just go on.

▲

If someone says, "Be realistic, be real," what they're talking about is something that they think is fixed, something that they think is permanent.

When I came into this company, people told me, "There's never been a black, female product manager," and "Black women don't do well here." And there are a lot of "realities."

When I first came to this company there had never been a black woman promoted to product manager across three levels. I just came in thinking, one day I'm going to be a marketing director. And when people said, "What do you want?" I said, "I want to run a division."

If you had asked me, "Come on, do you really think you're going to run a division?" I probably would have said, looking at that reality, "No way. This company in my lifetime is not going to evolve far enough for me to run a division."

I really believed that in my heart of hearts. But you never would have seen me acting like that or behaving like that or even saying that.

I was promoted, and people gave me negative information. It was a staff job. It was known as a "female job," and people would say, "I don't know why you would take a job out of line management and go and do the 'women's job.' They must be pushing you aside."

They'd give me all this negative stuff that was a part of their reality. And for me that job was the greatest opportunity. Get out of the division to rub elbows with really senior people so I could observe them and learn. And then demonstrate that I could do more than the "woman's job."

▲
If you don't like your reality, change it.
▲

If you're unhappy, change it, because reality isn't fixed and it's not permanent; it's temporary.

There's an aspect to reality that will be fixed if you want it to be, but it won't be if you don't.

▲
It may be the reality today, and it may take you longer than you want to change it, but you can change it.
▲

—*43-year-old Division President*
Consumer Packaged Goods Marketing/Manufacturing

The Secret of
Frontal Disclosure

If you don't have all the facts, say so.
They can always tell when you're lying.
(But they'll hardly ever tell you.)

▲

The thing that ticks me off the most in business is when people try to bullshit me. It's the only time I raise my voice.

▲

The thing a lot of people don't realize is that they can almost always tell when you're bullshitting.

▲

Bosses and co-workers can almost always tell when you're bullshitting them. A lot of times, though, they won't let on. And what's happened is that in one invisible moment you have destroyed their confidence in you and eliminated any trust they held in you.

And you'll never know how it happened.

This goes on so much. All day long. I find that a lot of people try to bullshit—I'm talking upper management, even. A lot of them bull-shit, too, from a lack of confidence and because they have a title that says they should have the confidence, that they should have the knowledge.

If someone walks in and tries to bullshit me, I'll throw them right out of my office. I'll tell them to come back when they have their facts straight. And I've unnerved people when I've done that. I'll be honest with them.

▲

There's one hell of a difference between, on the one hand, knowing the answer and, on the other hand, knowing only half the answer and making the rest up, hoping it will work. Believe me, you rarely fool anyone. And the moment you cross that line, you're dead.

▲

—37-year-old Senior Vice President
Women's Fashion Manufacturer

The Secret of
Personal
Limitation

The better you do, the better you'll think you are, and the more work they'll give you. Learn when to say "no" before you self-destruct.

▲

I've seen a lot of people screw up in both major and minor ways.

▲

One of the major ways in which I've seen people screw up is when they start to believe their own story. I hope I never do that because that's when you take the leap off of a cliff. That's when you take that opportunity that you really aren't qualified or prepared for.

▲

Career-step screwups happen when, rather than settling into something which they actually are very good at, people seek a broader, bigger base—the old term was the Peter Principle. I'm guilty of it as well.

I've had that experience. I tend to bite off more than I can manage.

When you perform well, the tendency is to constantly have more things thrown at you.

I've done it with people I've managed.

When they're good you keep giving them more things to do. When there are five people in an organization and one stands out as being exceptionally strong and one stands out as being kind of average, the one who's average gets very little to do, and the one who's very strong gets everything to do. The flow of work and the flow of opportunities tend to work that way.

▲

A tendency of people who screw up is that they tend to say yes. They take on more than they should and they burn out. The next opportunity is always flattering and always attractive.

▲

That's kind of the tendency I see with a lot of clients who become "deal junkies." Early on in their careers they're very good at spotting an undervalued opportunity about restructuring a company. Then they just keep taking more and more and more until they get to the point where they've taken on too much debt or more business than they can manage.

They buy something they really haven't studied carefully because they've become overconfident.

Overconfidence is another major pitfall.

My personal experience with it while I was rising up was when I was recognized as one of the young "rising stars" in the company.

I was one of sixty-five partners in the corporation, and the youngest. I was again encouraged to take on additional responsibility. It was never, "Well, you've done that job well; give that up and do this." It was always, "Take on this additional work."

Well, being ambitious and aggressive and liking what I was doing but wanting to do more, I accepted it.

And I spread myself too thin.

That's another characteristic that can hinder your growth—not being focused enough.

In fact, I was spread so thin that it hurt my performance across the board. Nobody there noticed it; I noticed it. Clients probably noticed it.

I wasn't paying as much attention to clients because I was paying more attention to administrating and managing.

I would have done two things differently. I would have not taken on the additional job for another year.

A year later, for the other businesses I was running, I would have hired or developed replacements who could have stepped into my role.

That's where I really screwed up. Had I done that and then taken on the new responsibility, things would have been fine because I would have had people running the other areas, and I still would have been influencing and controlling them.

—*37-year-old Senior Managing Partner*
Investment Banking Firm

The Secret of
Romantic Devotion

The more in love you are with your job, the more successful you'll be. If you don't love it, don't be afraid to leave it and find one you will love.

▲

It seems pretty obvious, but one of the most important objectives when you go into a career, or when you're looking for a job, or trying to figure out what you want to do, is to find something that you love to do. Because, at a minimum, you're going to spend eight or nine hours a day at your job.

If the average person sleeps another eight hours a day, he's going to maybe have seven or eight nonworking hours in the average day that he will not be at work.

So, essentially, for half of your waking life you're going to be at work.

▲

If you look at how you want to spend half your waking hours,

the last thing you want to be doing for that chunk of time is something that you don't enjoy doing.

▲

Since you're going to be spending that time anyway—and most of us have to—you might as well find something that you like doing.

If you're like most people, if you find the right job, you like it a little bit, and then you like it more, and then you like it for more than eight hours, and you like it for more than nine hours and more than ten hours. Pretty soon it becomes almost all-engrossing.

I think one of the themes you're going to find with successful people is that they spend more than eight hours a day at work and they love what they do. As a result, it's almost a self-fulfilling prophecy.

If you get into a job you don't like, you're not going to be very successful at it, no matter what somebody tells you.

▲

The real key to success is finding something you love to do. Don't let anybody else tell you what you will love to do. And if you don't love something that you're doing, don't be afraid to leave it.

▲

Don't be afraid to go out and find something else.

I'm sure you've heard many people say, "I was doing something. Then something came along, and either I lost my job or something unexpected happened, and I was forced to take a different path. And that's made all the difference." I think that's the key.

When you look at your future career or something that you're interested in, don't worry about what somebody else thinks. Listen to what you think yourself.

Listen to yourself to find out what you really enjoy, and go after it. And then when you make that decision, give it 110 percent. You'll find it's a lot easier to give 110 percent to something you're really in love with.

—35-year-old Senior Vice President
Global Mining and Minerals Company

The Secret of Enlightened Self-Actualization

Make sure you know what you don't know.

▲

One big thing I've observed about people, no matter where they are in the organization, is that the ones who succeed are those who really have a good objective, realistic understanding of their own limitations.

Some people just don't know their own limitations. They don't think about it. It's hard for them to think that they could be limited or weak in anything. You have to try to really understand and come to grips with what you don't like to do, what you're not good at.

You're better off taking a risk to do the things that you think you might enjoy, even though you haven't tried it yet and you don't know for sure.

You're better off trying to do the things that you think you're good at and that you're going to enjoy doing, because the enjoyment of doing something usually goes hand in hand with doing it well. If you're not enjoying it, that means you're probably struggling.

If you're not going to enjoy it, then you're just going to fuck up.

So realize what you can't do and try to think about where your skills and your enjoyments really lie. And try to do those things.

▲

One of the things that separates the early succeeders is that they're instinctual as to their limitations. I find that the people who usually succeed very well are the ones who know what they don't know.

▲

Even though they don't know it, they have a sense of what they don't know.

Some people just have an instinct, "Gee, I know a little bit, but I don't know a lot. I think there's a gaping hole here. I'd better get some help."

A lot of successful people that I know are not afraid, not insecure about surrounding themselves or interacting with very, very smart people.

▲

A lot of people who fuck up are the know-it-alls who don't know what they don't know, and haven't got a clue that they don't know what they don't know.

▲

—43-year-old Venture Capitalist

21

The Secret of
Sudden Destiny

Your career path may be determined by
a few critical decision points that can
appear without any warning.

▲

▲

**In every career there are critical turning points. If you don't
handle these curves in the road well, you can crash into the
wall.**

▲

Once I had just gotten this new group to manage. We were
profitable. Another group was not profitable. The head of this other
group, who was a sales guy, invited me to come to an early-morning
meeting.

This guy was fifteen years older than I was. Very sharp dresser,
very together. He was so tight that you could balance a pin on his
clothes. A very powerful presence.

All of his people were in the room, and so were our bosses. And
immediately my antennae were up: "What's going on here?"

He went through a couple of pro forma items on his agenda. And just in passing, he said, "By the way, I'll be reporting on the revenue for your group from here on out. And now let's turn our attention to item six on the agenda."

I said, "Excuse me?!" in a loud tone of voice. And everyones' heads turned. Like, "Uh-oh, now what?"

He clearly wanted to take over the financial responsibility for my group, so I would essentially have been reporting to him.

Had I acquiesced, had I just been unsure, had I been insecure, had I said, "Well, he's a pretty tough guy. I don't know. Do I want to deal with this? Maybe I ought to go to some friends of mine who are not in this meeting and ask them what they think I ought to do?" It would have been over. I mean, no kidding, it would have been over. I would have acquiesced in front of top management. In front of both of our bosses.

Instead, I said, "Excuse me? I didn't agree to that." And he said, "Look, that's just the way it is." And I said, in a loud, assertive tone of voice, "Like hell that's the way it is! Over my dead body, that's the way it is!"

Then one of the top management people got in and started refereeing this argument that was occurring in front of a fairly large audience of people.

We actually had it out right there, and I won. If I had lost or if I had said nothing, you wouldn't be interviewing me.

Basically, he figured I was a technical guy and I was too out of it to know what he was doing.

That's one of those critical career decision points, or action points, that are not very tolerant of you getting them wrong. It's like what you say when someone says, "Will you take on the management of this group?" or, "Will you take on this risky project?" They're waiting to see what you will do, and whether you're going to hesitate or not.

▲

This is more than just "He who hesitates is lost." It's not just hesitation; you've also got to make the right decision. If you don't hesitate and you get it wrong, then if you look at a career

as a series of decision trees, you'd be off on another branch, whatever the other branch leads to. You often have no idea when these critical decision points are going to happen.

▲

Most of our school lives are spent in what I would call soft environments. You can say, "Well, can I think about this and get back to you?" Or you can go back to the teacher and say, "Look, I've changed my mind. I really will do the report on Thomas Jefferson after all."

But in business often you don't get to change your mind. Sometimes your decisions are irreversible.

▲

You can think of your life as having alternative paths, and the reality that you're currently living in is the one that is the summation of all prior critical decision points. Had you veered left when you actually went right, you might be in a totally different set of circumstances.

▲

So there are a whole series of events that turn out to be important that we don't even mark as important. You can't do anything about some of those events. But I could identify half a dozen critical events that were clearly controllable and important career wise. And those are the ones you have to be prepared for.

—38-year-old President
Computer Software Company

The Secret of
Eternal
Vulnerability

The higher you go, the bigger the target
on your back. Don't ever lose your
"edge."

▲

Investment banking is driven by production—production of deals, production of revenues for the department as a consequence of deals and transactions.

Investment bankers are middlemen. We're there to motivate transactions between a supplier of money and a user of money, and it's broken down to that level. The level you rise to in an investment bank is to some degree influenced by production, not necessarily by management skills.

So that means you produce more and they pay you more.

Simultaneous to that happening, there are junior people in the organization who are being trained and who are learning how to produce, and as they become more experienced they produce more.

Management is always charged with finding the equilibrium between the number of senior guys we need who we pay a lot of money to keep producing, and the number of up-and-coming junior people who will work harder and begin to get the same production.

▲

As a result, the bigger (i.e., more senior) you are, the bigger the X on your back because there are always junior people running behind you, clipping at your heels, saying to management, "I can do what he does, what she does. Pay me more than you're paying me, but less than what you're paying that person, and you will get the same production results."

▲

There's a trade-off in investment banking between security and pay. You don't have a lot of job security because you're only as good as your last deal.

When I start losing that edge for whatever reason, well, then the X gets too big and someone probably overtakes me.

—40-year-old Managing Partner
Investment Bank

The Secret of Self-Annihilating Irrelevance

They're paying you to have a point of view. Make sure you have one.

▲

▲

I've had a lot of bad bosses. But through those bad bosses, I've learned how not to do things.

▲

I had one boss who was two rungs above me, had been at the company ten or fifteen years, was a vice president. I had thought, given this, that he was a pretty important person.

I happened upon a meeting for a special high-level assignment, and my boss was working on it with his boss, the guy three levels above me. Some commercials were being presented, and his boss asked him, "What do you think?"

I'll never forget this—it made such an impression on me—the guy had absolutely no original thoughts about it.

I thought, "Here is this guy being paid all this money in a business where you're supposed to be doing all this thinking, and he doesn't have a clue. What is his value?"

I remember the look of frustration and pissed-offness that his boss gave him. The guy wound up being fired within the year, and I got his job.

▲

You've got to have a point of view. Even if you are an "executor," there are ways to have ideas about executing things more efficiently. If you can't propose your ideas at high-level meetings, then let your boss know.

▲

I live by the rule of making your presence known and trying to be indispensable. I don't mean indispensable by spending twenty-four hours a day being glued to your desk. I did that at a younger age and don't subscribe to that anymore.

No one's actually indispensable. If I got hit by a bus, my company wouldn't fold. I know that.

It means standing out and having original ideas.

What it means is that it would make a really big difference if I was here or if I wasn't here, that our clients would really get upset if I left or if someone wanted to get rid of me. Therefore my bosses would give me what I want in terms of money or title or whatever.

Many people are too shy, afraid, or insecure to speak out. It's not enough to just know things or think them. You have to express them.

—29-year-old Senior Vice President
Communications Industry

The Secret of
Iconoclastic
Inquiry

Have the self-confidence to ask stupid
questions, and to tell them what they
need to know, not what they want to
hear.

▲

One of the greatest rewards is to study a problem, to work on it
over time, and then to be put in a situation with a large group of
professionals who are also very talented, and to be the lone voice in
holding a position—and then to find that you were actually right.
That's happened to me numerous times.

I was one of the six or eight people who were involved in CBS's
role in the start-up of what was then called Trintex, now called Prodigy.
It was 1984. I felt that the company didn't bring a lot of value to the
videotext business.

I said, "This is not a business." There's no product here; there's
no "there" there.

I was the lone voice. And one of the best days I had was when
the corporation pulled out of it and said that we bring nothing to this,

there is no business here, no one's going to use this the way it is. And Prodigy today is a totally different business than Trintex was.

▲

It's having the willingness to go against the wind, to be an independent thinker. People don't want to admit they don't understand something. They don't want to admit they're the one in the room who can't figure it out. It's the "I must be missing something, there's something here that I don't see" syndrome.

▲

You don't want to be the naysayer who becomes part of the past. Technology-driven products and businesses tend to be much more susceptible to that than others.

I think one of the mistakes a lot of corporate executives make—entrepreneurs tend not to do this because it's their own money, their own business—is they stop asking those dumb questions, because everybody wants to look smart.

You have to be willing to ask, "Why?" "What is this really going to do?" "Why are we doing this?" "What do you mean?" That's a very key point.

One of the frequent ways in which managers fail is that they lose the self-confidence to ask questions which run the risk of making them look stupid on the surface. You can become so caught up in your own myth, start to believe your own story so much that you can no longer not understand something.

▲

You have to be willing to risk making stupid statements in order to continue to succeed. Actually it's a continuation of self-confidence. You have to have the confidence to not know.
▲

—37-year-old Senior Managing Partner
Investment Banking Firm

The Secret of Controlled Fatalism

Optimism is great, but don't forget to keep a focus on the bad news. If you project too positive an attitude, you can lose credibility.

▲

▲

Being able to directly communicate good news and bad news in a proper balance is something I see with a lot of successful people.

▲

I've seen CEOs of companies who are very good that way. They tend to make light of the good news, and they tend to focus on the things that are potential problems or real problems. They're more problem-oriented. They don't sit around and think about the good stuff that's happening.

▲

Some people always give you the good news, even when you don't believe that's all there is. Because everybody knows it ain't always good news.

▲

They lose a little credibility with you, no matter how you're interacting with them.

Presidents of small companies who haven't done as well as they could have or should have tend to be the ones who tell you that everything's fine all the time or that things are going to be okay.

They don't think enough, or they don't communicate enough about what they're doing in trying to solve the problems. They're always giving you the good news.

Whenever anybody gives me only the good news, I know there's something wrong.

—*43-year-old Venture Capitalist*

The Secret of
Retail
Fundamentalism

The more front-line, "battlefield"
experiences you acquire, the more
successful you'll be.

▲

▲

**One of the keys to making rapid progress in a company is
having a real knowledge of the business. I mean understanding the business at a shop-floor level or at a transaction level,
depending on what industry you're in.**

▲

I was working in car dealerships and garages for ten years before
I ever stepped foot inside an automobile manufacturer.

I know what goes on in this business where the rubber meets the
road. I mean where real live people are buying and selling real live
cars or having them repaired.

I've stood across the counter from thousands of customers.

It gives me an insight to this business that a lot of the people who
probably have more traditional backgrounds don't have. You know,

go to school, get an MBA, go work for a big company—a lot of them don't know anything about the business.

Their perspective on the business is from a very lofty perch.

I know this business from the ground floor up. I know it from every nut and bolt, from real live customers buying and selling the product. It gives me an advantage.

I came here at thirty years old, but in the ten years I've been here I've had essentially ten full-grade promotions.

▲

Get out there—talk to your customers, watch them buy and use your product. Get your hands dirty. It will give you a real edge.

▲

—40-year-old Strategic Planning Executive
Automobile Manufacturer

The Secret of
Profitable
Proximity

The closer you are to the bottom line,
the more career leverage you'll have.

▲

▲

**I learned quickly that I had to get in a job where I could
demonstrate bottom-line results. For anybody, especially
women and minorities, I think that's one of the most important things to do.**

▲

If you're in a staff job, then you are more linked to the politics of
it all.

But if you can get out there and show that this is the profitability
that you've brought to the company, or here are some tangible
achievements that have happened under your leadership, then you
either stack up or you don't.

Your success will then be based on the results you've achieved,
and not the politics you've played or who you ate lunch with or where
you went to school.

▲

Find the bottom line, and tie your career to it.

▲

Ten years ago, if you went into the retail side of the banking business, boy, that was career suicide.

It meant you'd never be seen again, you'd never be at the corporate head office, and that's not what you wanted to do.

It's changed over the years. My management has become much more bottom-line oriented.

Now retail is the place to be, and it's where I am.

Once I learned what their sensitivities were and what they were putting emphasis and importance on, I knew exactly where I needed to position myself. I was able to move into a job that had bottom-line, revenue-generating impact.

—33-year-old Senior Vice President
Retail Banking

The Secret of Transcendental Perception

If others have the wrong perception of your job performance, it's your problem, not theirs. You have to fix it.

▲

▲

Too many people get too defensive when being criticized. Many of the people I've seen fail are the ones who get too defensive or emotionally involved in criticism or mistakes they make.

▲

You have a perception of yourself. And let's say everybody else's perception may be totally different. Now is it their fault or your fault? Obviously it's yours. They can't fix it. You can.

Really listen to people and don't get defensive about it.

Think about it. If that's their perception, that's your problem. Not theirs. Yours. You said it, and somehow that's the way they heard it. Even if you don't think you said it that way.

I say that to my vice presidents now all the time. They get very defensive about certain things that they might be challenged for. I report to a division president. He's very close to all of us, because we all worked very closely with him. He challenges me a lot about different people on the team. I share with them anything he says, because I don't want any secrets that are not necessary.

They get very defensive. I'll say, "Wait a minute, before you bother to get defensive, listen to the perception, okay? Because he has a perception about you. Not about me, not about him, about you.

"That's your problem. You have to fix it. Because if you don't, he's going to keep the perception."

So instead of sitting here freaking out and calling him a name, think about what you did that gave him the perception.

When your boss tells you this in a constructive format, listen.

▲

I've seen so many people not listen. All they've done is take themselves out of the company, the company that they wanted to work for. And even if you don't think your boss is right, they're your boss.

▲

You can change it by listening and reapplying. You can't change it if you walk around and say, "What the hell does he know?" It will be on your review next year, next year, next year. Again, that's the perception they have. You've got to change it, whether you like it or not.

Most people I've seen leave have left because they can't accept criticism.

I just had a young lady who had been here ten years, and she left. She worked for me for the longest time, but my boss above me always had a problem with her. His perception.

She didn't do anything to change it. I kept saying to her, "I know it's a perception. Maybe it's not even correct, but it's his perception. There are millions of people who see you every day. Maybe they all have a similar perception, too, okay? I don't have it, but that's me. And, yeah, I'll promote you as far as I can promote you, but how far is that going to be? He has the ultimate say."

Her problem wasn't the actual execution of the position at all, but people skills and general maturity. And she just wouldn't change it. She wouldn't accept the fact that he might be right. So now we're down the road ten years. People are getting promoted around her. She's sad, she's hurt, she's been used, she's been abused. But only by herself.

So I said to her, "The only person who's abused and used you is you. You've allowed it to come to this point." She never chose to go in and see him and talk to him personally about it.

It's so funny, because this last week we were in a meeting, and he said, "She never once came into my office and asked me, 'What's this perception you have about me? How can I fix it? What am I specifically doing that really twists your hair? Tell me.'"

But in order for her to seek it out, she had to accept it. And she would never accept it. So she would never seek it out to fix it. And whether you like it or not, you have to accept it. And if you think it's wrong, okay, maybe this person's perception is wrong. But you have to fix it.

▲

It's your job to fix the perception.

▲

—37-year-old Senior Vice President
Women's Fashion Manufacturer

The Secret of
Heroic Adversity

Turning around troubled situations is an
increasingly valuable career skill.

▲

▲

**The ability to go in and turn a company around or turn a
product line or a division or a bad situation around becomes
a real tribute to the individual. That's a very good mark to
have on your resume.**

▲

It is inevitable that companies will stumble. It's a cyclical thing; we
all have run into difficulties. There's a long laundry list of companies
that were the blue-chip, premier companies of United States industry
but that are today scrambling around to find out what they can do to
be profitable again.

Even though our company is growing, we still have to take a lot
of hard positions with cutting back, layoffs, cost containment, consoli-

dation. So I don't think anybody is detached from the potential of having something like that occur.

The one-time shot, the great innovative design or new product development, is the root of American business and should not be trivialized.

But the shortfall of that is that after you've attained it and you're involved in a competitive market situation, it's only the person who knows how to really run the business who's going to keep the thing going.

▲

It's only the person who's been through the tough times and the street fights and all of the tough things that companies are being asked to do today, who can respond to a tough competitive situation or a market slowdown.

▲

The guy who lives on great successes with new product development, all he knows how to do is spend money on R&D and hire salespeople.

The guy who has had to try to keep a company alive in a less than acceptable growth environment is going to be far more valuable in today's troubled business environment because all companies are facing very, very tough decisions with staffing and cost containment and expense controls and everything else.

—38-year-old President
Diagnostic Imaging Manufacturer

The Secret Law of Inverse Credit-Grabbing

Management usually finds out who's really performing. The less credit you try to grab, the more you may get.

▲

The more mature people in business realize that if you put your head down—don't piss anybody off from the political perspective, do a great job, and don't look for credit—people recognize it and you'll be rewarded.

▲

Probably the biggest thing I've seen that's a career killer is burning bridges.

▲

It's small world that we live in. Any time you don't act with integrity and honesty and you burn a bridge with somebody, it's going to come back to haunt you somewhere in your business career.

▲

I've seen people burn bridges by taking credit for things that they didn't do. You're in a group setting and somebody stands up and takes credit for something that either you or someone else did.

▲

I had that happen to me at a company where I used to work. A guy tried to steal credit from me. When I left, he was the only individual who did not come up to congratulate me upon my new employment or come to the going-away party they had for me. And it's just one of the little things you kind of look at and say, "That's not someone I want to be associated with."

The firm I used to work for is doing some business for us, and I've told them that if that individual gets anywhere near our account they'll lose the business.

Management knows who does the work; they know who comes up with the important contributions. The credit will come your way in some way, shape, or form.

▲

The more insightful, impressive leaders will never pat themselves on the back. They'll always give the credit to those who work for them.

▲

That's why I said I think a lot of it links to maturity level. That's the difficult balance.

Part of my job is to take no credit.

I've got a great team of people who work for me. I'm at a position now where I am more of a facilitator; but as to production of the actual work, my team's doing it.

One of the most important things I try to drive across to them is to say that you're the guys who deserve the credit. You're the ones who are doing the work. And I can only be successful if you're successful.

—*32-year-old Senior Vice President, CFO*
Management Services Company

The Secret of Emotional Detachment

Know when to stop over-internalizing work problems and stop taking everything so personally.

▲

One of the reasons I did well was that when I got out of college and started working, work was my life.

I didn't feel like I was particularly good at "the boy thing" and relationships, and I guess I felt pretty good at academics and work. That's where I spent my energies. I put in long hours and got emotionally involved in my work.

I was once in line for a promotion and I really thought I deserved it. An older colleague and I were driving to a client. I knew he was a big supporter of mine, and we got along real well, and I was counting on him to say, "You're absolutely right. You deserve to be at that next level."

He didn't. Instead, he said, "You're not ready for that next level, but you can get there once you learn to separate yourself from business and not internalize and take it personally as much as you do."

I said to him, "You're absolutely wrong. If I do that I won't be passionate anymore."

He said, "You're full of shit. Trust me on this one. You will be. All it means is that you won't allow your own personal shit to get involved in the work as much."

▲

He was telling me to be mature—to pick and choose my battles better, to see things from a higher plane, to remove myself to see both sides of the issue before jumping in and voicing an opinion, to try to see the bigger playing field.

▲

He was really right. I didn't lose my passion. When things went wrong at work, I learned not to take it personally, not to go home and agonize so much.

—29-year-old Senior Vice President
Communications Industry

The Secret of Androgynous Management

If you can combine the best qualities of both "matriarchal" and "patriarchal" management styles, you'll gain a major career advantage.

▲

▲

Business today is moving from a strictly patriarchal to a more matriarchal philosophy. So people with the best characteristics of both philosophies will probably do much better.

▲

It's not just because there are more women in the workforce.

It relates to the new methods of doing things more efficiently. When you look at the qualities of teamwork, process implementation, operating systems, sequencing, nurturing people's organizations and projects, those are more matriarchal qualities than patriarchal.

To compete, you've got to be good at those things. It's not that women are forcing this change; it's the changing business methods, the new systems and processes we're using today to be more successful.

▲

A lot of times we men are thought to be running around with a "ready, fire, aim" style of management. Shoot before you think. Sometimes it's true. Hopefully someone with perhaps a more "matriarchal" attitude comes along and teaches us how to do things better. And "matriarchal managers" have things to learn from the patriarchal side, too.

▲

Both can be valid, and each can learn from the other.

Perhaps we should all become androgynous!

Because you'll never get away from the importance of decisiveness and action to move business forward. At the same time, once you've made a decision, if you don't have a system to process it and the teamwork to make it work, you'll fall down on the tactical side.

—39-year-old Senior Vice President
Consumer Packaged Goods

The Secret of Cultural Dissonance

If you find yourself in the wrong corporate culture, you owe it to yourself to find a new one.

▲

▲

One of the things I've seen that stops people's careers is an inability of some people to work within a given culture.

▲

This tends to hit some of the brightest people I've known.

You should not stay in a firm where there's a discontinuity between your personal style and values and the firm's style and values.

You can work to change it, and maybe it's enough to stay and say, "I'm going to try to change it."

I've seen people who have developed very negative attitudes about the firm, even though it's providing their source of livelihood, because at a gut level there's a discontinuity in the value system and style. And their careers stop as a result.

They're not able to give it their best effort because what's always gnawing at them is the fact that they don't really fit.

They really shouldn't be here.

I've seen people who stay. They've stayed their whole careers, and they get to a certain level and just stop. It has nothing to do with their intelligence or their potential contribution or anything else. It's just that they didn't fit. And that's what stopped them.

▲
_____

If you honestly can't work within a given corporate culture or believe that you can't have enough of an influence to modify it, to be fair to yourself you should probably find another company to work for.

▲
_____

—40-year-old Strategic Planning Executive
Automobile Manufacturer

The Secret of Personal Re-Engineering

If you want to change jobs, consider shopping around a business plan instead of a resume.

▲

▲

I am comfortable breaking convention at any time. I probably take it too far, because I intentionally try to violate the norm.

▲

I was working at an old-line Wall Street investment house, and doing well there. In 1990 I determined that there was a highly profitable new niche of financing emerging in the market and nobody on Wall Street was properly addressing it.

I left my company. I put together a fifty-page business plan for a new operation that would capitalize on the trend by operating as an autonomous new business within an existing investment house.

I took a risk. I had enough money to pay the rent for a while, but there was no guarantee that anybody would back my business idea on my terms.

It took me three months to put the plan together. It was just me and the plan—nothing else. So I started shopping the plan around Wall Street, to the various companies I thought might have an interest in it.

During this time I was offered a job at a traditional investment bank with a guaranteed salary and bonus, so it made my decision difficult. On the one hand, I had a guaranteed offer and on the other hand, I had total risk with the business plan I was shopping around that I liked.

I took the entrepreneurial route. I decided to make it as easy as possible for my potential "employer/backers" to accept the risk of starting up my new operation. I offered them this deal: I'll set up an autonomous group, run the show, do all my own hiring, not report to anybody but the top at your company, use none of your resources. In return, if I hit agreed-upon revenue and profit targets, I split the profits with you.

If I go into the red, you fire me. That's the deal. It was written right into the business plan. Needless to say, that put a rather enormous amount of pressure on us to perform!

Luckily, we've done quite well, exceeding our plan, and are now in our third year.

—*36-year-old Senior Managing Director*
Wall Street Securities Firm

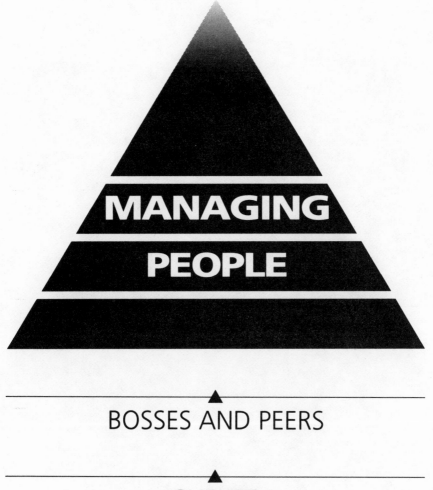

BOSSES AND PEERS

CLIENTS

SUBORDINATES

The Secret of the
Mentoring Mosaic

Everyone in the organization, from top to
bottom, can be your mentor.

▲

▲
You should cultivate a variety of different kinds of mentors.

▲

When I was in school there was a lot of dialogue among the women students about "How are we going to get mentors because there aren't women who can mentor us? Will men take the risk of mentoring women?"

After a while I realized that mentoring was different than it had been defined.

▲

The common definition was that high up in the organization somebody had a vantage point that could help you see things which from your limited sphere you couldn't see. What I recognized was that mentoring was in fact very different. I now call it a "mentoring mosaic."

▲

As an example, one of the guys here is a moving guy. He happens to be black, as I am. When I first came in I used to talk to him and he'd talk to me. Just hello and good-bye type of stuff.

When I got promoted to my first office, which was my second promotion, he moved all my furniture, and he's moved me ever since. He moves everybody. He said to me, "Let me give you some good advice. You see those senior guys over there in the corner?" I said, "Yeah." He said, "You look at their offices. Their offices are neat. Now that you've got this office I want you to straighten up everything."

My first attitude was, "Thank you very much, Bob, but I'm the Harvard MBA." And then I realized that this guy had moved every executive in this building from the time they were probably assistant product managers. And what he thought he was doing for me was giving me some good advice. And it was.

Ever since, I've tried to figure out who can give me advice.

Some of that advice is advice on presence, and some is advice on how to "manage up."

And it doesn't necessarily come from people who are sitting in lofty positions.

The secretaries in this company have experiences. They've seen people who've moved around, and there's a lot of information that you can just pick up in casual conversations, through observation.

I probably have gotten more from unsuspecting portions of my mentoring mosaic than I have from people who over time have said, "Hey, you're a good person. I've been around longer, I'm more senior, let me help you." It's harder to cultivate those relationships. More people seek them out. Most people ignore some of the other good sources of help that are around them.

I always tell women and minority MBAs, "Don't ignore the likely sources of help." If you're fortunate enough to have someone who will extend themselves to you, great.

But if you can't find one or two people right away, don't think that you can't get help. Because you can.

—43-year-old Division President
Consumer Packaged Goods Marketing/Manufacturing

The Secret of Solicitous Engagement

Four of the most powerful words in business are "What do you think?"

▲

▲

What I find interesting is that the really successful people ask other people for their advice.

▲

They may accept it or not accept it, but they don't act like they're the world's smartest guy.

They're not bashful to ask you, "What do you think? Do you have any ideas?"

That's a powerful phrase.

▲

That one sentence "What do you think?" can open up a whole new world of knowledge to someone.

▲

A lot of people don't ask that of people inside or outside their own discipline.

They're afraid to. A lot of people think, "It's my job. I should know this."

You have to realize your own limitations. You try to be confident about what you are capable of doing. At the same time, you don't want to come across like you know something you don't know. You want other people to know that *you* know you have limitations.

▲

It's important that, in a very delicate, tactful, effective, positive way, you have other people perceive that your limitations are recognized by you.

▲

You want others to know that you're going to outgrow those limitations, and that you know what they are. You don't want to be viewed as being someone who's half-cocked and reckless, and who's going to walk over a lot of land mines because you haven't been there.

You want people to be comfortable that when they're walking with you, you're not going to step on a land mine. You're going to be smart enough to carry that metal detector.

—43-year-old Venture Capitalist

The Secret of Perpetual Skepticism

The next most powerful words in business are "Why are we doing this?"

▲

Part of what separated me from other people was that I had no preconceived notions of the business world. I was not impressed with the structure of Price Waterhouse and its prestige because I never knew about it or cared about it.

I went in with a real "Brooklyn attitude." I was constantly asking, "What are we doing this for?"

▲

That exact question is the one that I use most today. "What are we doing this for? Why are we doing this? Why are we doing it this way?" If you try to boil it down to a phrase, it is challenging convention.

▲

A lot of times there isn't a good answer, and obviously anything you're doing that doesn't either make money or make customers happy you should reexamine.

You have to be careful with the tone of the question and how you phrase it.

You can ask either superiors or subordinates the exact same question two different ways and get a 180-degree difference in reaction. With a superior, you're either insightful or cocky. With a subordinate, you're either motivating or a son of a bitch.

▲

Instead of saying, "What the hell are you doing that for?" the key is to be somewhat self-deprecating—"I don't understand. Explain it to me. I'm turning over the power of this issue to you because you're obviously the expert."

▲

—38-year-old Senior Vice President, Sales and Marketing Consumer Product Company

The Secret of
Delicate Assault

When you attack convention, be careful
how you tone the assault.

▲

▲

**Never be afraid to challenge an idea, but be sure you first have
credibility, and then be careful that you present the challenge
in not too aggressive a tone.**

▲

The world's slightly different for women and minorities, especially
if you have a powerful and aggressive personality, but women and
minorities need to figure out what the rules are and play by those rules.
You work to change those rules, but you've got to play by those rules
during that time.

I find frequently that men who are in positions higher than I
am are threatened by someone beneath them in the organizational
hierarchy who is comfortable challenging their thoughts and ideas.

Frequently you see people taking positions that may be opposite from yours, or maybe just not supporting you in certain ways, simply because they are in some way threatened by you.

You may be in a meeting where you challenge someone else's comment, and you may be offending a different person sitting at the table without even knowing it.

I think that you have to build credibility first before you challenge, by proving that you're a good worker and having proven results.

Understand the people you're challenging. If you're going to challenge somebody's ideas, you have to be willing to listen to their ideas and modify your own.

To the extent that you might be willing to give a little ground on issues that are not important for you, then you're going to win on the big things.

> **—*33-year-old Senior Vice President Retail Banking***

The Secret of Narcissistic Arrogance

People care less about you than about what you can do for them.

▲

▲

I'd say arrogance is probably the biggest career killer, because nobody knows everything. Arrogance coupled with the inability to listen. Listening is so much more important than talking—listening before you speak.

▲

Boy, you see it all the time in investment banking.

You have senior people in investment banks thinking they kind of walk on water.

In a previous job I once lined up a small company to do a financing. We had basically already won the business, and all we had to do was make a presentation in front of the Board of Directors, along with the other investment banks who were pitching the deal.

We were well on the track to having the business, but we could not get our senior people to take this seriously enough to understand the company.

They just blew in with a very arrogant kind of approach. They didn't know much about the company, didn't really do their homework, and just expected their own titles to carry them, whether it was Harvard Business School and First Boston Managing Director or whatever.

Instead of asking questions—to demonstrate our ability to serve that company—they ended up so caught up in their egos that all they could talk about was themselves, how great a company we were.

We had an hour, and we should have said, "Look, you are a great company. You're small, but you're growing. We're behind you. We love the fact that you do this, this, and this. We think your management is great, and we want to be your financial adviser through the '90s."

Or, "One of your concerns has got to be the yield on your cash portfolio. We've got some ideas for you."

Instead, it was, "You've gotta do this with us. There's nobody else on the Street like us. We've done so many deals. We are so great, you can't afford not to do business with us."

So the potential client, who looked like he was getting physically ill, cut the meeting short at about twenty minutes, and said, "Well, thank you for your time—and good day, sir."

We absolutely got it handed to us.

We were left out of the deal and told they didn't want to talk to us ever again.

It's a mistake to rely too much on your resume, on what you look like on paper, as opposed to what you can prove you can do for somebody at the moment.

▲

Don't come in saying, "Let me talk about me for the next half hour." It's just worthless.

▲

Anybody in a service business who starts out that way is a real dead-ender as far as their career goes.

It becomes harder as you become more and more successful to

remember that; since you're so happy with your own accomplishments, you really want to talk about them.

But the people who really continue to succeed are those who are able to continue to listen.

—34-year-old Chief Financial Officer
Broadcasting Company

The Secret of Presumed Incapability

Assume that many people may think you're incompetent until you prove otherwise.

▲

This is important for everyone, and especially for women and minorities: the presumption of lack of competence.

It makes a huge difference when you walk into a room and people assume you know what you're doing, versus their assuming you don't know what you're doing.

I've had people say to me, "Gee, I was surprised how feminine you were." Particularly when I started, the image of the woman professional was a "battle-ax in a bow tie." One of the biggest hurdles was to get people to recognize that I had some degree of competence.

▲

My own experience is that you can't spend a lot of time worrying about whether it's fair or not. It isn't. You just have to deal with it.

▲

You have to have the patience to keep at it with logic and rationale and demonstrating your capabilities. You can't necessarily change people's prejudices, but most people are willing to make an exception for the individual if you just keep at it.

▲

One thing I have found helpful is never to confront someone by saying, "You're not giving me a chance to prove my competence." Most people get very defensive. You may just have to realize that you have a higher hurdle to get over than some other people.

▲

I have had a lot of jobs that require me to present things to big groups of people.

And you can tell when people are in the "show me" mode and when they are really listening to what you're saying.

I have gotten to the point where I can tell when people turn. You get sensitive to body language, to the kinds of questions they ask.

I know instantly when I walk into a room. When I know people are in the show-me mode, I put on an "Okay, I'll show you" presentation.

It's much less of a conversation, and more, "I've got thirty minutes to show these people I've got something to say." That's a different dynamic than, "Okay, we are two competent peers having a discussion."

In the latter, there's a lot more "I don't know, let's talk about that" that's permissible. In the former case, in my experience you can't ever say, "I don't know" until someone is willing to deal with you as a competent individual.

You gotta show 'em. Not in an obnoxious sense, but in a self-confident sense.

—37-year-old Vice President
Global Telecommunications Company

41

The Secret of Cross-functional Sacrifice

Taking a view broader than your department's can score you valuable points.

▲

▲

Whenever you're in a cross-functional situation and you have four or five people in on a project from different departments with a common superior, don't solve your problem. Try to solve your boss's problem, even if it means your department will take a bath.

▲

Look at it from his or her position—managing four or five competing points of view and thinking, "He wants this, she wants that. Now I'm going to have to say, 'You—no, you—no, you—yes, you—no.' "

Then you come in and say, "In this case, what's good for my division isn't going to solve the problem because the overall solution is way over here and *my department will have to make a sacrifice.*"

Since it may come out that way anyway, if it's the right answer and you're the one who's going to have to give in, you might as well get credit for forming the problem.

You get two benefits from that. First, your boss is saying, "Here's somebody who knows how to think how I think."

Second, he or she knows you're going to take a hit, and will try to be fair to you next time.

Now you've got a win instead of a loss, and it's better than being dragged into submission later.

—39-year-old President
Consumer Products Company

The Secret of Invisible Subculture

Make sure you understand the hidden network of relationships in your company before you speak out.

▲

Many people who are viewed to be shining stars in an organization tend to be viewed that way because they have a certain amount of brashness to them. They will assert their ideas; they will articulate them. All of those things are really positive. Those are also the exact same kind of things that can get you into tremendous difficulty and trouble.

▲

You need to learn—and this comes with time, and after having made a few very critical political mistakes—that you need to listen and you need to have the background on a lot of subjects before you just jump in.

Your tenacity, your personality, the things that have made you come to the attention of the people you most want to impress—these things also could become your Achilles' heel.

You have to learn not to take every issue to the mat.

I worked for the Walt Disney Company for a few years. It's a very wonderful company; it has a tremendous external persona. A very tough organization, internally. And very political.

I made so many mistakes there. They weren't performance mistakes.

They were all political mistakes.

The first one was in an Executive Committee meeting. I had been on Executive Committees in the past, and I felt like those were really pretty open forums and that you could speak what was on your mind.

After about three months they asked me to give a review of the people who were my subordinates, so I did.

After the session was over, someone took me aside and said, "I don't know if you know, but that was a senior vice president's brother-in-law you were blowing away."

So knowing the background is very important. By the way, I ended up ultimately becoming fairly close to the person. And I came to realize that he also thought his brother-in-law was kind of a jerk. But I had never encountered an organization where there had been family members involved in the company on that many levels.

They were not so much within one department, but you might have someone who's a senior executive in one division who's married to someone who's a senior executive in another division. So you had to be very, very careful.

I should have looked for the assessments of that particular individual that had been given by my predecessors to see if there was already a trap being laid, that this person wasn't perhaps the best performer, versus just coming in and saying, "Well, I've seen this guy. He's worthless. We need to cut bait here."

Clearly, learning the art of taking someone out and trying to get the other side of it, and questioning, that's part of doing your homework, doing the background check. "How is this person regarded in the organization? Who's he attached to?"

Believe me, immediately after that meeting, I went back to my office and said to my secretary, "I want a list of every person in this organization who's married or related to someone else."

Sure enough, there were connections I never would have made. Married women who used their maiden names, people who were so-and-so's brother, so-and-so's cousin. A lot of organizations don't allow it to happen. But inside this organization it was clearly allowed to happen.

That was one I was definitely unprepared for.

—38-year-old Senior Vice President
National Retail Store Chain

The Secret of
Critical Mass

Your boss doesn't promote you.
Everyone does. If you don't treat the
masses with respect, you're taking a
major career risk.

▲

▲

**One of the things I've noticed that has caused some people
to have problems with their careers is being too aggressive
and/or career-oriented.**

▲

Many times they step on people in order to get ahead, and you
can basically see that everyone around tends to turn against them,
including the people who work for them. To me, it really boils down
to having some patience, as well as respecting people.

There is nothing worse than some of these people who talk down
to their secretaries, then cater to those people they think may be able
to give them an extra kick in their career. They don't recognize that
most of the time people see through that, and very easily.

I think that it's the supervisors, in many cases, who see through it, as well as the peers of that person. In most cases, they don't want to have anything to do with them. They don't want them on their team. They work with them only because they have to, in order to somehow uphold the company team spirit.

▲
_____

You have to be somewhat humble and, first of all, try to learn the business, try to obtain respect from the people you're working with and the people you're working for and the people who work for you. Because those same people are the ones who will help promote or encourage your career.

▲
_____

You just never know. I saw a situation where a manager was really, really tough on his secretary, for no reason, just because she was a secretary. He talked down to her and ordered her around.

Little did this manager know that her secretary happened to be the best friend of the CEO's secretary. When this secretary went to lunch with the CEO's secretary, she said what a jerk this particular manager was and how she's treated. That got passed on to the CEO.

Those kinds of things happen quite frequently. You just never know when you're dealing with people how it's going to ultimately affect your career.

—*35-year-old Senior Vice President, Finance*
Transportation Company

The Secret of Humanitarian Restraint

If you cross the line between losing your temper and humiliating someone, you can do irreparable damage to your career.

▲

I saw an individual in my peer group lose their temper over a relatively minor issue with a subordinate.

This person was using abusive language and semi-publicly humiliating the subordinate. It was in a one-on-one meeting in the individual's office.

But it just so happened that one of the key executives walked around the corner at the time this individual was doing it.

This person's career literally stopped.

This happened seven or eight years ago. I don't think the person has made a single career move since. This company won't tolerate treating people badly in a personal way.

▲

This is only business. It's not worth killing anybody over.

▲

What it demonstrated more than anything else was the person's inability to keep their professional life in perspective.

The people you work with, and particularly subordinates, are kind of entrusted to your care.

There's a social network or fabric, and you really don't have any right, for any business objective, to violate the basic covenant of social decency.

▲

People lose their temper once in a while; that's fine. But this was to the point of public humiliation of subordinates. I don't give a damn what the business objective is; you have no right to do that.

▲

—40-year-old Strategic Planning Executive
Automobile Manufacturer

The Secret of Infinite Benevolence

If you're not good at managing people, you may survive only as long as your numbers are good. When they go soft, you could be doomed.

▲

▲

When people are really, really smart, and are very good at delivering business results, but are miserable with people, they run into big trouble sooner or later.

▲

They tend to get things done through people in very negative ways, and people hate working for them, and they degrade people, insult people, treat them rudely—all the things you wouldn't want in a manager.

Everybody puts up with it to a point because these people are very smart and they deliver results, and people sort of brush off the fact that the behavior exists.

Then these people get to a critical point. Depending on the function and depending on the individual, that critical point is different.

What happens is one day someone stands up and says, "This

person is a schmuck. They can't deal with people. In this organization you've got to get stuff done through people."

Their boss tells them, "Yeah, you've got to do better on this people thing." But they never beat them up on it. They never really make them feel the impact of it.

Then all of a sudden they come back and they say, "Hey, you're not going to get promoted to GM," or "You're not going to get promoted to marketing manager until you're able to deal with people or until you fix this interpersonal skills problem."

Then the person goes bonkers; they say, "Well, I deliver results and I'm smart." And then the boss tells him, "Yeah, yeah, yeah, that's all true. But now the next level requires that you're able to do this with grace and charm and inspiration and motivation and you don't do that."

Then the person blows up. The person doesn't understand what's happened.

Unfortunately far too often people don't get the right input until it's too late.

Those people get "nuked" eventually. You have people who rise to the top who have those characteristics, but we lose some terrific people in the process.

We often don't get on those issues early enough and really help people understand the importance of leading, motivating, inspiring, and positively influencing those who work with them, and what kind of behavior will get you where you want to be in the long term.

▲

You may deliver the quarter; you may deliver the year. You can deliver a couple of years, but eventually you beat out of your good people the creativity and spontaneity. And eventually they leave. They don't want to be working in that kind of environment.

▲

—43-year-old Division President
Consumer Packaged Goods Marketing/Manufacturing

The Secret of Interdependent Achievement

Even the most brilliant strategic move can be derailed if you ignore teamwork.

▲

▲

It is rare that someone's career is meteoric and doesn't hit plateaus, walls, curves, zigzags, changes, tumults.

▲

At the young age of thirty, I was country manager for a major foreign market, a country of over 100 million people.

We had a fairly large business, and we were determined to restructure it. I was absolutely determined that I was going to do this, and do it in the right way. I went about it with a personal vengeance and commitment that I never had had in my life.

It was one of those things that you do at a young age that can be a "career definer." I dreamed this, lived it 100 percent. I was street savvy and analytical. I was hard-driving.

I eventually restructured the business, which required ridding us of a joint-venture agreement with another major multinational company.

I negotiated it away from them. It was very complicated legally. They lost millions of dollars; we lost literally no dollars.

I got the brand ready for a complete relaunch in one of the largest markets in the world.

I presented that plan to the president of the company, had a terrific meeting where everyone patted me on the back and said what a terrific job I had done.

Then, as I walked out of the meeting room before catching a flight back, someone asked me to see someone in personnel. So I did.

This person, whom I had never met before, started telling me about some of my personal traits that people weren't excited about.

An inability to listen. Inability to connect personally. I was arrogant, independent, knew better, and gave the perception that I wasn't listening or had some other motive. "You never look people in the eye when you talk to them."

Then he announced they were going to have a new job for me!

What hurt me was my desire to hit the finish line and not really be concerned about how I got there.

▲

It was one of those classic cases where sometimes thinking about the end line, the touchdown, and not thinking about your partners or your compatriots can be deadly. In today's workplace, getting teamwork and support for projects is critical. The people who are ultimately successful are the ones who are able to get support, as well as results.

▲

—39-year-old Senior Vice President
Consumer Packaged Goods

The Secret of
Interactive Nobility

No matter how well you've mastered a technical area, you may still have to place a huge premium on interpersonal skills.

▲

It's much more important today to have a business perspective as well as a technical perspective. It is also much more important to have good interpersonal skills and to be able to work within intracompany relationships as a critical element of your job.

▲

It is not enough to just be a "techie"; it is not enough to just be a superstar. What is important is that you need to have the ability to understand the overall business, and you need to have the ability to work with others and to have a team mentality.

▲

The costs of "genius," the cost of issues that are related to the management of highly technical but independent-minded people almost becomes too expensive to deal with.

As a result of that, although you need those personalities, the people who will advance and the people who will succeed are the people who have not only some technical skill but a business overview and the ability to work with others.

▲

It is critical to be a team person in today's environment. The tougher the business situation, the more you have to behave as part of the team. You can't have a separate agenda.

▲

No matter how technical your job is, if you're a litigator or a research guy or a "bean counter" or whatever, you still have to pay very close attention to interpersonal skills.

—38-year-old President
Diagnostic Imaging Manufacturer

The Secret of Dysfunctional Empowerment

Always assume you can do your job better. Make your bosses tell you how.

▲

▲

Take the total quality management approach. It always gets to what do your customers (or your bosses) need? What do they want? It's incredible how rarely people ask, "How am I doing?"

▲

"How do you think I handled that meeting?" Or, "Gee, what did you think of that report I did?" I'm not talking about the person who is constantly saying, "Tell me I did a good job, boss."

A lot of people say, "Gee, I never got a performance evaluation." Well, did you ever go ask for one?

Did you ever walk in and say, "What can I do to be more effective?" Or, "Gee, you know, I think I really screwed up on this last deal. What do you think I did wrong?"

I've done that. Absolutely. Now, I can remember a few times

where I walked out not very happy. In one instance, it was a pretty miserable couple of weeks, because I thought I was doing a great job.

I was getting signals that the guy I was working for was less than 100 percent enthusiastically supportive of what I was doing.

Yet I kept going back to my job description and thinking, well, they want me to do this, this, this, and this. And I'm doing all of those things. And I'm doing a great job. So why isn't this guy giving me a few "Atta boys"?

Finally I set up a meeting with him. This was not a very communicative person, and a lot of bosses aren't. A lot of people aren't. I said, "Well, I just wanted to have a mid-course chat. How am I doing? I think I've done these things well."

He says, "Yeah, I'd agree with all that. But you're doing the wrong things. These things aren't important to us. We don't really care if that gets done." I said, "But my job description says this." He said, "I don't care about the job description. That's not what is most important to the company or to me at the end of the day. You should be doing more of the following."

I don't think he had ever articulated in his own mind the heart of it.

Sometimes, as a subordinate, unless you make it easier for them to give you feedback, in their own mind they're saying, "This doesn't feel right. I know her job description says this. I know that she's doing everything that her job description says, but how come I don't feel good about it?"

Sometimes you have to give them the opening.

Because they might also think, "Oh, gee, if I tell her this, then she's going to be upset." So I think you've got to go in every once in a while and say, "How am I doing?" Or, "How do you think I handled that?" Or, "What can I be doing better?"

▲

Solicit feedback and make it easy for them because it's really tough for your boss to give you negative feedback. This way you're enlisting the support of your boss.

▲

Most bosses are going to be quite willing to help if you say, "How can I do better? How can I help you better? What do you want me to do and why?"

"Gee, do you think that I'm being too aggressive on this?" Or, "Do you think I'm going into enough detail on resolving this thing?" Or, "Am I being responsive to your needs?" With questions like that, they're a little bit more comfortable coming back and saying, "Yeah, you know, you are a little bit short-tempered . . ."

There was a time in my career when I thought, "Oh, God, I'm making no progress, I'm just replowing the same old ground," or, as they say sometimes, "Five years of experience, one year five times over."

One of the big differences now is that I'm much more willing to walk in and solicit that input and solicit the help, not putting the whole burden on them, because that's really tough.

▲

Make it easy for them to give feedback. "Tell me what I can do" is awfully open-ended. But being specific, asking, "Well, what about this? Should I be doing more of this? Or am I doing enough of that?" gets their support, because most bosses want their people to do well. And they're not going to abandon you then. Just the fact that you care enough to do that goes a long way.

▲

—39-year-old Business Unit President
Transaction and Information Processing Company

The Secret of Graceful Resilience

If you're being hammered by a boss, don't rule out the possibility that he may actually be right; assume total ownership of the problem.

▲

▲

The people I've seen self-destruct around me in the past few years are people who are extremely defensive, people who hold onto their position because it's their position and refuse to be accountable.

▲

I think that unless you're surrounded by real ogres, there's a level of humanity you have to project. People listen if someone says, "You know what, in retrospect it was a bad judgment. You're right. And I own that. How can we fix it?"

People tend to be much more supportive of that. At the very least they're not going to see you as an asshole. It's the people who become defensive, who deny accountability, who even deny that a mistake was made, who will tend to self-destruct.

If you're being scolded, getting angry and antagonistic or shouting back are really bad moves.

You don't have to turn into a Milquetoast doormat, but there's a level of calm and personal dignity that's very important to maintain, especially when you're the one who's been wrong. If someone is chewing you out, stand there and accept it, take it like a grown-up, and perhaps even say, "You know, you're right!"

▲

If you're being accused of doing something that you did not do, definitely stand up for yourself. But if you're being taken to task for something you did, absorb it. Because, you know what—it's an opportunity to learn.

▲

If you deny it, you'll never learn. You'll never find out what your mistake was and not do it the next time. How are you going to grow?

The people who self-destruct are the ones who are defensive, argumentative, and pains in the ass.

▲

When you start to smell that you're having trouble, it's important to reach out for help.

▲

Call in your superiors and say, "Hey, something here's not working out." Be the first one to call it. Be the first to acknowledge it. You're taking the weapon away from the enemy by giving it to them.

If you say to them, "Look, this isn't working, I'm having a problem. Help me," then it's not just you holding on to something.

I had an experience just yesterday where I was being raked over the coals, and I turned to my boss and said, "You know what, you're right! This is a judgment that we made a year ago. Perhaps in retrospect it was wrong, but we made this judgment and now we have to fix it."

It deflated him entirely. He said, "Okay, now you have to fix it, and this is your period of time to fix it."

Nothing is 100 percent great all the time. In America we tend to seek perfection and think it's a great personal failure if we haven't achieved it. We think that our career has to be golden and fulfilling 100 percent of the time. Nothing is.

It's like a marriage. Sometimes you wake up and you're in love and it's great. A lot of times you're just married! It's also true of your career; a lot of times it's not particularly pleasant. So what? GET OVER IT!

—36-year-old Senior Vice President
Media Company

The Secret of
Self-forgiveness

You're not perfect. The faster you forgive
yourself for making a mistake and learn
from it, the less damage it will do you.

▲

Don't pretend you know everything.

Part of it is that sense of emotional centeredness that allows you
to say to yourself, "If I make a mistake it doesn't mean that I am a
fuckup. Therefore I can own the mistake." If you're afraid and terrified
to tell yourself you've done something wrong, you're only going to
make it worse for yourself.

▲

**That's the hardest thing—to look in the mirror and say, "I
made a mistake. I did the wrong thing." It's okay. Forgive
yourself. Then you'll be able to "own" your mistake, work with
your peers to fix it, or cut your losses. The worst thing you can
do is get into a position where you refuse to see that a mistake
has been made, because you'll get in deeper and deeper.**

▲

I'm wrangling right now with an issue. A year ago I was part of a group of people who made a decision that may have been a huge mistake; it cost us a fair amount of money—not a huge amount, but a fair amount.

I now have a few months in which I have to try to salvage the situation. I might not be able to. I have to be prepared to forgive myself for that judgment. And that's hard. But if I don't, nobody else will.

I might forgive myself and my boss still won't, but at least I've forgiven myself. If I don't forgive myself, you'd better believe me the boss won't forgive me, and the level of blame will carry over and undermine me completely.

▲

We have a mental image that our culture gives us to live up to, that we should be kind of "Bollo Suave/Charlie Girl": smooth, easy, "Kinda Free, Kinda Wow." Look at all the advertisements of young execs—beautiful, preened, never have a run in their panty hose, getting in and out of cabs—who are these people? It's a burden to carry that around as an expectation for yourself.

▲

Those of us who came of age in the 1970s had, on the one hand, the Charlie Girl and, on the other hand, the "woman with a Y" feminist separatist saying, "Well, fuck you all!" Who am I going to be? The feminist separatist or the Charlie Girl? The truth is somewhere in between—neither, or both.

I also have to put it into balance with things I've done that have been very good decisions so it doesn't wipe me off the planet. The temptation is to think, "Oh my God, everything else I've done that had any value for the company disappears." Well, that's not true either. I'm also doing some things that are very good.

So, okay, I may have made a doozie of a mistake. I was part of a group of people who made that doozie of a mistake. We'll do everything possible to correct it. I feel terrible about the fact that I miscalculated, but in the face of that I feel, well, take it on. Own it.

It's hard. I am wrangling with this right now. And the biggest enemy is myself. I want to fall into a pit and say: "Oh, my God. I'm a fuckup!"—"I don't know what I'm doing!"—"I don't deserve my job!"

Why do I feel that way? Because I have an expectation of being perfect. An expectation of being the Charlie Girl. And I'm not.

**—36-year-old Senior Vice President
Media Company**

The Secret of Perceptual Confrontation

If superiors have the wrong perception of your performance, don't let it fester. Quickly muster the guts to ask them what the issues are and tell them you're going to try to fix it.

▲

I had a boss whose boss had very strong opinions on people and situations.

It was real clear whether you were on the "in team" or not. And it was real clear to me that I was not on the in team.

In big meetings he liked to play games with people, to show off in front of large crowds. You'd think, "I'm going to go in and take my public flogging now."

He started beating up on me in a big meeting over something that was really just a philosophical difference. He was yelling at me, and I just was appalled.

I was incensed. So I sat there, and I realized I'm not going to argue with him 'cause I'll get fired on the spot. But I walked out of there and everybody knew I was really angry.

One of the guys on the in team who was a friend of mine came in to my office and said, "This is the way he is. Don't let him get to you. Don't overreact to him." And I said, "Bullshit, I don't have to take this." He said, "Look, fine, but shut your mouth and deal with it."

I decided I'm going to get on his calendar for lunch, and I'm going to directly say to him, "I really want to personally understand what your issues are with me and my performance, because I want to succeed here. I've had a good track record, and I believe I can do what you need to have done in this division, but unless I really know what's at the heart of your concern about me, I can't succeed."

I thought that this was a high risk, and I really got myself psyched for this lunch.

▲

He was brutal. He told me exactly what was on his mind. He told me I was smart, but not as smart as I thought.

▲

He said, "I think you're far too detail-oriented." And I'm thinking, God, I've been pressuring myself to get this detail. I hate it; I'd much rather tell you intuitively that this is the right decision.

Some of it was probably right. I had come out of a division where when you went into meetings you had to have a lot of data; they wanted a big thick deck and nothing was taken for granted. If you made an assertion, they wanted all twenty-seven backup points.

He really liked a style where you come in and you make your assertion. If he asks some questions, then you'd better be prepared. But he doesn't want to know from all of your detail.

▲

I said, "I'll fix what I have to fix because I won't succeed unless you support me. I'm determined over the next few months to do whatever I can to address all of your concerns."

▲

I said, "I'm not trying to be flippant, but I've known myself thirty-five years. And you've worked with me for less than a year, and I really believe that some of these issues are valid and I'm going to do everything I can to fix them. And other issues are things I have to show you and I want to work to do that."

It was very hard to actually face him and do this, and then to sit there and have him sneer at me and say, "You're not as good as you think you are."

I felt really shitty for a while. And then I thought, okay, this is motivation. Either he can defeat me, what he believes about me is true, or what I believe about me is true. One of us is going to wind up happy!

I got three or four promotions after that famous lunch.

▲

It's tough, but you've got to not be afraid of situations where you can be committed enough to hear whatever the horrible news is so that you can deal with it. It's a demonstration of courage.

▲

—43-year-old Division President
Consumer Packaged Goods Marketing/Manufacturing

The Secret of
Critical Separation

Whenever you're criticized in business it may be ten times worse than they tell you it is. Don't take it personally.

▲

▲

The ability to take criticism is a very key trait. People don't like to give criticism, and people don't like to get it. But, I'll tell you, it's better you have it than you don't.

▲

Everybody's always going to tell you nicer than it is. Even your friends.

Whatever they tell you, it's probably worse.

You need to know not to take it personally, because we all criticize each other fairly constantly.

A couple of years ago there was somebody at this company who had a "big idea." The rest of us thought it was dangerous and would not work, and we tried to question him, but he wouldn't discuss his plan because he wanted to "own" the big idea.

We told him this project has a lot of legal risks and technical risks, the chances of things going wrong are good, so let everybody take a crack at criticizing and maybe improving the chances. Don't keep it all to yourself, or when it goes down you're going to go down with it.

He thought we were out to get him.

He was wrong. We just thought it was a potential disaster for the company. And it was. He isn't here anymore.

—39-year-old President
Consumer Products Company

The Secret of Psychotic Displacement

Try to disconnect yourself from the mood swings of an abusive boss.

▲

Maybe your boss has a personality that doesn't match yours.

Is that an evil person? Well, maybe, but maybe not. And even if you're up against somebody who is a real abuser—and there are a lot of those out there—you can choose to stay there or you can choose to leave.

▲

Turn it around in your head so you're not the victim.

▲

There's no point flailing against the sky. It's very easy for people to set themselves up as the victim, to say "this is an evil place." Well, no, it's just a place that's not for you.

If you find yourself trapped in a situation that's not a happy one, decide that it's your choice and claim it, as opposed to feeling, "Oh my God, I'm stuck. It's evil; look what they're doing to me."

It's very simple. A good boss is somebody who allows their people to fail. A bad boss is somebody who shames and blames.

There are two kinds of bosses—ones who realize that everyone in the company is going to make a mistake at some time, or ones who expect perfection.

Blamers and shamers are counterproductive. They terrorize their staff so that they're afraid to do their best work. Good bosses are the ones who allow for a margin of error, who encourage people to come forth and experiment and show their best selves.

I've had "terror bosses." It hurts. It's terrifying. It's horrible. You have to realize that these people are not going to change.

These people are who they are, for their own reasons. You're not going to change them. I decide to absorb their behavior emotionally in a different way.

I can give them that power to make me feel like a turd, or I can say, "I feel bad. I don't like it, but this is not the truth of who I am. I made a mistake; I'll make it better next time."

I believe in psychotherapy. If you find yourself working for an abusive boss, find yourself a good shrink! It's very important to not get attached to the praise of the "shamer/blamer boss," because he's also often the praiser.

It flip-flops. You're the golden boy or girl today, and you're a piece of turd tomorrow.

▲

If you get overattached to the praise, then you are totally vulnerable to the blame, and I promise you it will be around the corner. The blame can wipe you out.

▲

Try to have a healthy detachment to all that stuff, and feel good about yourself at your current level. This is very, very hard.

These personalities are everywhere in corporate life because often these are people who have achieved a lot of power.

People at the top are not particularly happy themselves. They're seeking success of a very big order to make themselves feel better, and as a result they're not particularly kind to others. You have to fortify yourself against it. It's going to happen a lot. And it's never going to feel good.

**—*36-year-old Senior Vice President
Media Company***

The Secret of Protective Insulation

It's also your job to protect your staff from an abusive boss, to protect the work they do for you.

▲

▲

It's really your duty as a manager to at least try to shield your people from irrational emotions and reactions that might be coming from above.

▲

But you also need to realize that there are limits and that you can't always protect them.

I had a boss who could be furious about something. He would go to a person who had nothing to do with that problem, and blow off steam at that person over a much smaller issue, because, for whatever reason, he was afraid to encounter or approach the person who he really had the problem with. There was a lot of displaced anger.

It happened quite a bit. I remember several occasions when he was starting in on me, and I would just stop him and say, "Wait a minute. How can you be so mad over that issue? What is it that's really bothering you?"

A lot of times, little dinky things would become major, major issues. I'm thinking, "There's no way that the president of a company can be that mad over the fact that it took an extra day for our marketing director to do his expense report. Who cares in the scheme of things?"

Let me tell you, I tried very hard to insulate my staff from his outbursts, because I think that's crucial. I see it as part of my job to create an environment for my staff to flourish and do the best work that they can possibly do, to be rewarded for that and to feel they're appreciated.

Unfortunately, my boss's personality prevents him from working through a formal chain of command. He's going to go wherever something is bothering him, and he's going to deal with that person whether they report to him or to somebody who reports to him or are the receptionist who answers the phone. He's not a bureaucracy-oriented person. He goes right to the point.

As a result, I've found it exceptionally difficult to insulate my staff from him, even though it's something that I strive very, very hard to do. And I don't think it was coincidental that in late 1988 two of my four direct reports resigned on the same day. The reason that both of them cited to me is that they just couldn't deal with working for my boss.

I've actually been chastised about this by my boss; he would yell at me that I was too protective of my staff. That was because my first reaction to his outbursts was, "No! You must have gotten your facts wrong." So I guess he was right, I became very defensive of my staff. I had to be.

**—34-year-old Chief Financial Officer
Engineering Company**

The Secret of Counterintuitive Ambition

Don't automatically avoid working for a "bad boss": You may get major credit for improving the situation. (You may even get his job.)

▲

▲

I've always wanted to work for "difficult bosses" and "difficult clients." Give me a challenge. Give me a way to justify my existence. Give me a way to let them know three months down the road that I already matter, I count, I stand out, I'm making an impact. If I'm working on a business that's automatically growing 15 percent a year and everyone is getting along just wonderfully, what the fuck do they need me for?

▲

I want my presence to be known. It's okay to work for a bad client. Then I can improve the financials, or improve the work, or improve the relationships. I can get my fingerprints on the wall. I don't look for nasty situations, but I look for situations that need improving.

I once went to work for a guy who was a complete and total slimebag.

Why did he get as far as he got? I guess partly because he had a British accent and that has a real effect on us Americans. Second, he had a relationship with a big, important client that went back to their days together in London.

He pretty much had free rein because his boss was distracted with running the office. Meanwhile, he was running the business into the ground and creating a real mess financially.

The account was $2,000,000 in the hole.

The stories I heard about him were probably the tip of the iceberg. I'd heard he was totally political, talked out of both sides of his mouth, was a whore to the client, gave them anything they wanted instead of what was good for their business.

At the time, I was in a different part of the company and wanted an opportunity to grow, and it was hinted to me that it might be good to work for this guy because he'd been doing it for a very long time and would eventually get tired of doing it.

My peers said, "You're out of your fucking mind" to consider working for such a nasty client and boss. I went out to lunch with him to see if it was something I wanted to do, and I was honest with him. I said, "You have a terrible reputation." I wanted to see what he said.

I figured if he could convince me otherwise, that was fine. He didn't convince me otherwise, but I was impressed with the fact that at least he acknowledged the problem.

After I started working for him, a lot of internal people started realizing how much things were improving, how much better things could be. I wasn't walking around saying, "This guy is an asshole"; but people saw how different things were, how much better they were being treated.

Things started catching up with him. People started hating his guts after hearing really slimy things he was saying behind their back, a lot of real shitty things.

Eventually he was asked to leave, and I got his job.

—*29-year-old Senior Vice President Communications Industry*

The Secret of
Therapeutic Terror

A maniacal boss can teach you valuable
lessons about being "buttoned up."

▲

I once had a boss who was brilliant but also maniacal—a real crazy man. He was the best and worst of bosses in one.

In order to get him to make a decision you had to be completely knowledgeable about anything that you would present to him, every specific detail of the proposal. You really needed to know every implication of whatever you were trying to accomplish—legal, financial, etc.

If you didn't, he would end the meeting immediately. He'd say, "You're not prepared. Come back and see me some other time."

▲

**If you came in with an idea he didn't think was good, he'd
spend a half hour yelling and screaming about how it was the
stupidest idea he'd ever heard of and how could you possibly**

be so stupid as to propose it. From the perspective of learning to prepare myself even better for meetings and decisions, it was great to work for him, although obviously there were some downsides to that relationship.

▲

He was a terrible boss in that the level of anxiety he created in the workplace was extraordinary; his people would not make decisions or propose decisions they thought were the best decisions, but rather those they thought he would say "yes" to.

The level of emotion and anxiety and the tone of conversations with him would always be extremely loud and extremely aggressive.

In order to participate in that process, you had to get yourself fired up and really rise to a high-pitched level of aggression and emotion anytime you would meet with him.

My blood pressure rose daily.

He would manage by fear. It's a dangerous way to manage. You end up having your people make only easy decisions, out of fear of being intimidated by you.

The aspect of working for him that I liked was that you were forced to prepare to a level that made you feel comfortable that you were making the right decision. However, those decisions that you eventually made would not always be the best decisions because you were working for someone who was so smart that he would think of so many things he'd get himself tied up in knots.

He'd say, "Okay, I understand that, but what if . . . ?" That "what if?" might have a one in 100 or one in 1,000 chance of happening, but he had the terrible combination of being both extremely brilliant and extremely paranoid, and he had a significant fear of failure.

He didn't ever want to make a decision where someone could question whether or not it was the right decision.

▲

He taught me you shouldn't walk in the door until you're prepared to answer any possible question about the project at hand, even if it means staying at the office till midnight,

working through the weekend, whatever it takes. It means being buttoned up—having all the answers.

▲

I've seen people not be buttoned up and it's been a disaster.

I was in Japan four months ago doing a deal with a local theater owner. Across the table were a manager and several of his bosses. They started asking him questions. He didn't have the answers.

They slammed into him, over and over. It was a brutal thing to see.

—39-year-old President
Pay Television and International Home Video

The Secret of
Deferred Justice

Bad bosses are not immortal. Often they
self-destruct.

▲

▲

**The basic thing I learned from the worst boss I ever had was
that no matter how much I tried, I couldn't please him. And
I ended up quitting the company because of him. Soon after,
they fired him.**

▲

He wanted to sell computers like ladies' ready-to-wear. The day
I met him, we had an argument over that very point. I told him you
couldn't sell computers like ladies' ready-to-wear. And it was pretty
much all downhill from there.

He had a habit of going out and sitting in front of a store I was
responsible for, and he would take out a little portable tape recorder.
And he'd talk about the store. He'd go into the store. He would make
notes as he talked about it. "This looks good. This looks bad. I don't
understand why they're doing this."

He would bring those back and he would transcribe them. Anything that was negative about the operations side of the business, he would send to the president in a memo, never anything positive.

It was almost like, "I'm trying to go out and get you fired," as opposed to sitting down and saying, "Hey, you know, I noticed this little display wasn't quite the way it should be." He did this to other people in the company, too.

One person he did this to sent him a note. It said, "Fuck you. Stronger note to follow."

He and I obviously got off on the wrong foot, and there was literally nothing I could do.

So far, at that point in my career at that company, I had done almost nothing wrong. And all of a sudden, I could do nothing right.

I tried and I tried, and there was nothing I could do.

My conclusion at that point was that A) I felt like I still made good decisions, and B) I still had confidence in myself, although they were shaking it. So I thought, well, if that's the way it's going to be, then I'd have to go. I have to leave, because this guy is in my way.

And eventually I left the company.

I came back a year later. Because three months after I left, they fired him.

**—39-year-old Executive Vice President
National Retail Computer Chain**

The Secret of Proactive Disobedience

When a client or boss wants something, don't be afraid to tell them they're wrong, or they actually need something else.

▲

▲

In any business you have to deal from strength, and the minute that people perceive that there's weakness, you're in real trouble. Weakness can be saying yes too many times.

▲

You're supposed to be the expert. I've seen traps happen all the time where in order to hold on to a situation, you start going along with the dictates of wherever the client is. You're no longer advising, you're executing—and you've lost your main role in the process.

Now there are some people who aren't too rational, and if you don't do exactly what they say, maybe they're going to fire you, but that's inevitable anyway. If you're good enough, you don't need to have clients like that no matter how big or powerful or rich they are.

No matter how difficult they are, most of the people—most of them, not all of them—will respect you. There are some situations that are just not salvageable. But you've got to stay in your role; the minute you don't, it's over.

When you're really busy you've got to be real careful. In this business, you're dealing with people's dreams much of the time. If you really feel you know the marketplace and you're very sincere and you look at someone and say, "I won't do that, I can't do that, that'll never happen," they look at you like you've taken the air out of their balloon. It's tough. You've got to be real careful when you tell people no.

If you can convince people that what they want is not what they want, and steer them in another direction, that really helps you as much as it helps them because no one's wasting time.

**—36-year-old Executive Vice President
Hollywood Talent Agency**

The Secret of Structural Sensitivity

Be sure you know what you're doing before you go around your boss. You may wind up ticking everyone off.

▲

▲

I've seen people go around their bosses and get in trouble.

▲

I used to work at Arthur Andersen, and the way it was structured from the bottom up was staff, senior, manager, partner. One staff person kept going around the senior to talk to the manager and tried to show that they were doing a wonderful job.

They didn't understand the relationship that the senior and the manager had. They pissed off the senior for obvious reasons.

They eventually pissed off the manager, too, who didn't want to deal with this situation, who didn't want this person coming to him all the time outside the regular chain of command.

This person didn't understand how much these people interact with each other and what kind of reputation you get really quickly without even having worked for a lot of different people, because all of these people talk to each other, all the time.

You see that a lot—people really trying to hustle and prove themselves, and they end up making themselves look bad and kind of like an ass-kisser a lot of times. If you're going to run around the hierarchy, or do an end run, you'd better be sure that you know what the relationships are because it very well might backfire.

▲

I've seen smart people who really want to succeed build a reputation like that, and they don't get very far. Two years and they're out. All of a sudden they're shot out of the saddle. They look like the only survivor of a ten-car pile up; they're just bewildered: "What the hell happened to me?" They just didn't realize the way things worked. There is a definite hierarchy and political structure in large organizations. When you are in that type of situation you've got to understand and respect it.

▲

—29-year-old Vice President and Controller
Environmental Services Company

The Secret of Selective Insubordination

Sometimes, though, you have no choice but to go over your boss's head.

▲

I spent some time working in Atlanta and then went to London for two years. Some of the people I was working with had a very parochial attitude about the U.S. being the only place in the world, and why would you ever want to go to London. I went against one individual's guidance.

Upon my coming back, he decided that he was going to make my life a living hell.

For almost a year he put me through a real hell. I mean it was miserable.

Part of it was because he had told me not to go overseas, and I went anyway. It's tough enough being out of the U.S. work environment for a couple of years and then to try and jump right back in the saddle.

▲

He effectively did everything in his control to either "test" me or to try and push me into a position where I'd fail.

▲

The personal pain and terror that I had internally got to the point where I was waking up in the middle of the night in fear. The anxiety and the pressure were tremendous. It was more than I've ever had anywhere, in anything I've done.

I have left only one job in my life, which was probably one of the hardest things I've done because I'm a fairly loyal person, and I never quit anything. So I'd be damned if I was going to quit.

My only other option, because it had gotten to the point of my not being able to deal with it, was to go in and confront the situation. I felt that I couldn't communicate with the person I was reporting to, so therefore I was going to go to a higher authority and try and elevate it.

I decided to walk in to his boss, my boss's boss. I said, "This isn't going to work. I can't work under these conditions. We either need to change them or I need to find something else to do."

Naturally what happened was that he went to the guy I was working for and mentioned it to him. I got called into his office, and he and I spent probably fifteen minutes circling his desk. As he came around one end to come and talk to me, I went around the other end to say, "Hell, no."

I ended up having a conversation with him, and the tension was eased as I stopped working for him as heavily as I had been. I think he understood the situation, and the pressure stopped. It became much more of a team effort.

—32-year-old Senior Vice President, CFO
Management Services Company

61

The Secret of
Perpetual Looping

Tell your boss about everything
important. Never surprise him or her.

▲

▲

**The two "land mines" that I've seen that you most want to
avoid are, first, you never want to embarrass your boss. Second, you always want to make sure your boss knows everything important you're doing.**

▲

The worst thing that can happen is for your boss's boss to say to
you, "What about this?" because he found out about it from somebody
else, and your boss didn't know.

The biggest mistakes I have made and some of the biggest mistakes I've seen other people make are when you're not forthcoming with information, particularly to your boss.

—39-year-old President
Pay Television and International Home Video

The Secret of Diplomatic Counterterror

When dealing with a terrorist, credit-grabbing boss, give him what he wants, but discreetly communicate your accomplishments to others.

▲

I had a boss ten years ago who I'd say fits the category of "the worst boss."

He was an incredibly insecure person.

He was constantly concerned about taking credit from everybody around him. Not necessarily doing all the work, but making sure that other people believed that he did.

I had to spend a lot of time shielding my people from someone who was not very in tune with the business. He had a tendency to want to walk in and out of it so he could pick things up to get credit for them.

He also was the kind of person who didn't trust other people, who was constantly checking up on people, on what they had done.

He was looking to prove that they weren't successful or didn't do something well.

▲

I do think that you should inspect what your people do to a large degree, but there's a line between making sure things are getting done and that you're getting results, and looking for people to do wrong.

▲

I think people felt he got pleasure out of finding that someone didn't follow up on something, or that something wasn't done as perfectly as it should have been. It was really a bad environment.

I did a fair amount of closed-door confrontation with him, because that's more my nature.

I do believe very strongly that in public you support your boss.

And, in fact, I spent a lot of time supporting him, actually, even outside of the small environment we were in while I worked for him.

Because I think that's the only way you can be effective.

In a sense, I looked for kudos to get for him so that he could feel better and look better.

Because if he didn't look good, we'd look like jerks, too.

Did he appreciate my efforts on his behalf?

Not in a million years.

I don't think that he knew then or would ever recognize that people were doing things to try to make him look good, because it was not in his nature.

But I would make sure that I had enough relationships with all of the people around him and above him, so that I wasn't really completely reliant on him.

▲

I had enough ability and enough smarts to have people around him and above him who knew what I was doing and knew me.

▲

—39-year-old President
International Hotel and Resort Chain

63

The Secret of Tactical Counterassault

If you're being unfairly attacked, go to the source and calmly confront them.

▲

▲

You can't go around selfish bosses. You almost can't get the work done because they want to take all the credit for it. Those are the bosses who are most threatened by good performers. They don't have the self-confidence to deal with it.

▲

I had one instance of this.

We had a certification process for salespeople. Sales management had to be certified, and I happened to be on the board that did the certifying.

This person in management who was my superior came through to be certified, and his application clearly failed by everybody's measure.

Of course, he was very upset and blamed it on me because he had always felt threatened by me.

He decided that the way he was going to deal with this was to make it his mission in life to sabotage my career.

When we rate and rank people, we have large sessions where all the managers come together and talk about their subordinates.

That occasion provides a forum for somebody who wants to be very damaging about somebody else. There are a lot of people listening. If good things are said, it can advance your career. If bad things are said, it can damage your career.

So he set about using these forums to say very damaging and very untrue things about my capabilities. I happened to have a friend in the room who told me this was happening.

And, frankly, the way I ended up dealing with this was going into this man's office, and I guess the best way to say this is that I threatened him.

I threatened him in the sense that I said that I knew what he was doing. I had friends in the business who knew what I was capable of. I was going to be around a long time, and I thought he should reconsider what he was doing. And he did.

▲

The lesson I took from that situation was that you have to confront people who are trying to damage you in some way.

▲

It's interesting. I've had some wonderful mentors, but I do believe that in the end you have to manage your own career. To me that means that you have to be willing to confront situations head-on because no one else is going to do it for you.

If he had continued to try to "get me," my recourse would have been to go to his peers with whom I had created good working relationships and enlist their aid, so that other people would be aware of what he was doing, people who had the facts and who were prepared to stand up for me.

I think that would have been successful. Generally for everyone who is willing to sabotage careers, there is someone who is willing to stand up for the facts.

We never spoke of it again, and then I moved to another division and quickly surpassed him. After that happened, he was peaches and cream.

—37-year-old Vice President
Global Telecommunications Company

The Secret of
Savage Retaliation

Wait until they hurt you twice before you strike back.

▲

If you're working with good people, everyone notices when you solve problems.

Your supervisors say, "This person knows how to get things through the system."

Your peers say, "I want to do things with this person; I want to be an ally. I'm going to help this person because he or she is going places."

People will like you and respect you, and you'll get more access, more information, and be invited into more problems.

But there's another side to it. It totally reverses if you're working with "pricks."

Some people are threatened by other people's accomplishments, so if you find out somebody next to you is sabotaging you, and you're getting continuously screwed, you can only turn the other cheek for so long.

▲

You can't let yourself be a patsy. You have to fight back. My rule is to wait until they torpedo you twice before you nail them, because the first time could have been a mistake.

▲

If it happens a second time, you go to their office, shut the door, and say, "I know you're screwing me, and if you do it again, I'll take my gloves off."

—39-year-old President
Consumer Products Company

The Secret of
Strategic Exposure

Don't forget to try to get "face time" with
your boss's bosses—that may be where
the real decisions are made.

▲

▲

**Early in my career I was friendly with all of my peers and the
people one level up, but that's not where all the decisions
were made.**

▲

The decisions were made by people four levels up.

If all they saw was me working hard in my cube, and they didn't
have a sense of my personality and my style, I wasn't going to go
anywhere.

Early on, I couldn't separate being a suck-up and managing up.
I had a hard time with it.

Because I thought, gee, if I was in the general manager's face, I
was really being a suck-up, and I wasn't going to be a suck-up. I was
really opposed to that sort of behavior.

I was ready to be promoted to the first bonus level, and it was a big promotion. A position came open and I really felt I deserved it. They brought someone in from another division in June. And I got promoted in November.

But that was a long four months.

So when I went to talk to my manager, I said, "Look, tell me what I need to do to get this promotion."

"Oh, you're ready for it but we just have one concern. It's just that you don't interject that well."

And I said, "Well, what do you mean by that?" He said, "Well, we want to feel like you're a member of the management team, and we think that you sort of see yourself as a part of the proletariat."

I didn't like the language choice, but that was the image. He said, "You're a good team leader. The support people like you, but you've got to sort of rise above it. Now you have to be seen to be on the management team."

The point is that managing up for me had been an issue. And I thought I had gone a ways, but I had a ways to go, in their minds, in order to get to the next level.

▲

Managing further up than I thought turned out to be very important.

▲

—43-year-old Division President
Consumer Packaged Goods Marketing/Manufacturing

The Secret of Discreet Power-flirting

If you're going to flatter your superiors,
try to be subtle about it.

▲

There's ass-kissing that goes on all the time everywhere in different ways.

A lot of people who really fuck up a lot are the ones who are obvious about their ass-kissing and don't know it.

We had a partner who did that, and all the other partners knew it. He was ass-kissing a more senior partner who had responsibility over promotions.

For example, we would have a partners' meeting off-site someplace. And he'd be stupid enough to say, where others could hear, "When are you and I going to go fishing?" It was just so obvious.

He had told everyone else that he thought the more senior partner was not so great and that he didn't even trust him. Why would you ask someone to go fishing with you if you didn't even respect him or like him?

▲

Everybody does it. They're doing it in different ways. If you're going to do it, don't be so obvious about it. Although you may be getting somewhere with the one you're ingratiating, you're going backward with everybody else who sees it.

▲

And you don't realize it.

—43-year-old Venture Capitalist

The Secret of Preemptive Alliance

Don't just manage your boss—manage everyone else's boss, too. Forge alliances with the people you don't report to.

▲

▲

You have to manage not only your boss, but everyone else's boss, too. In other words, if you're a director of sales, there's no reason you shouldn't be trying to "manage" the vice president of operations, in the sense that you try to build a productive relationship with her before you need her help.

▲

The successful salespeople probably have a close relationship with people not just in sales and marketing. They've built strong relationships with the service people; they've built strong relationships with the development people, senior and junior.

You've got to build those alliances throughout the organization, not just vertically.

You've got to always look at it from their shoes. Understanding what the other departments go through on a day-to-day basis is critical. It's empathy for the other person and what impacts their livelihood or their side of the business.

The bottom line is empathy. You've got to understand your internal or external customers' needs and concerns and wants.

—34-year-old Vice President, Client Services
Information Services Company

68

The Secret of Disarming Desperation

Asking for your boss's help isn't always a sign of weakness. In fact, it can be a good way of deflecting a crisis.

▲

▲

There's a smart way of engaging your bosses in solving problems. It's also a smart way of "positioning" a problem so that it becomes a joint problem to be solved, not just your own.

▲

It's also a good way of delivering bad news. This technique is simply asking for your boss's help.

Most everyone in business has a quirk that they want to help and teach people—this is true of everyone, including your boss.

What you need to do to win their respect is, instead of walking into their office and saying, "We've got a problem," say:

"I need your help on something."
"Do you think this is the right way to do this?"

"Can I get your insights on a problem I have/a situation I'm facing?"

"How would you handle this situation?"

"Have you ever experienced something like this? If so, how would you have handled it?"

"What do you think of this situation?"

"I need your point of view on this."

"I really need your advice on this. Can I run this by you?"

What these phrases do is enable the boss to get involved on your side of the problem before it becomes a disaster.

It shares the responsibility for fixing the problem with him or her. It may save you time and a lot of grief later on. You might learn something.

And it's also an effective way of delivering bad news.

▲

How you manage bad news is often affected greatly by the delivery. It's often all in the delivery.

▲

I asked my boss for help just this morning in a similar way.

I was able to do it because we have a relationship of respect. I was able to engage him as a partner, not as a potential adversary down the line if the problem were to get out of control.

▲

If you approach your bosses and peers as if you always want to learn and since everybody wants to teach, you're going to learn a lot more and be more effective.

▲

—37-year-old Senior Vice President
Women's Fashion Manufacturer

The Secret of
Insubordinate
Clarification

Never do what your boss tells you to do.

▲

A lot of bosses say, "I tell my guys what to do and they do it."
Bosses like to say, "Do this" and "Do that."
That's not reality.

▲

You get all kinds of strange directions from your boss, from excessive rigidity to insufficient information. It's important that you clarify what you think they said to you and what you're actually going to do.

▲

You need to say, "I heard that. Let me just get this right. You told me to do this. I understood your reason was that. What I'm going to do, now that I've heard the general assignment, is go off and check these three things.

"I'm operating under these assumptions, and if they don't turn out to be right, then I presume I'm going to do this or that, and I'm going to come back and tell you."

You have to do this without being argumentative, of course.

This is very helpful to bosses.

It enables them to say, "Ah, I know what you're going to do now."

—39-year-old President
Consumer Products Company

The Secret of Targeted Love-bombing

The more you publicly praise your people when they deserve it, the better work they'll do for you.

▲

▲

Of the people that I've known who are successful, one common trait is that they all seem to have been quick to give other people credit where credit was due.

▲

They're the biggest cheerleaders—for other people.

It works because it makes other people feel good about what they're doing. If any person in the organization does something, he or she knows he or she did it. And when credit is given by someone who is in a more senior position, they're recognized.

Very few things can be as effective as long-term motivators.

If you're going to be successful, everybody around you has to do what they're supposed to be doing. And they have to be successful. If at the end of the day, you don't keep the people around you motivated, they won't do a good job, and then you won't succeed.

▲

Don't ostracize anyone in public when he or she hasn't done a good job. Do that in private. And when people in the company have done well, give them credit, and credit them when there are a lot of people standing around.

▲

That's the best way. Whether that person's there or not.

—43-year-old Venture Capitalist

The Secret of
Vertical Radiance

If you let your people shine, their
brilliance will reflect on you.

▲

The most rewarding experiences for me have been when my staff
has made presentations to large audiences, including our national sales
meetings, with my input and guidance.

▲

**I've been able to watch people grow and improve themselves,
and that reflects well on me.**

▲

People who have failed in this organization have been micro-
managing, controlling types who are either insecure or unable to recognize that other people may do things differently and may make
mistakes.

You need to give your staff the rope to go and try out things that maybe you wouldn't have thought of, recognizing that sometimes they'll perform assignments as well as or better than you, and that sometimes they may not perform as well as you would have liked.

Delegating gives you the opportunity to expand your own responsibility into other areas because you don't have to handle every minute detail of every project.

People who aren't able to do that don't succeed, and the people who are able to do that have the benefit of developing people, watching them succeed, and probably being recognized for that, too.

The best way to help you grow in your responsibility is to push responsibility down.

The first time you do that with someone you don't know that well, you ask yourself, "Do I trust this person? Are they going to do the kind of job I would do? Are they going to make mistakes? Am I going to look bad?"

▲

But you have to give people the opportunity to shine.
▲

—33-year-old Senior Vice President
Health Care

The Secret of Motivational Nurturing

The more you show your people you care for them and connect with them as human beings, the more successful they'll make you.

▲

▲

The attitude I've always tried to project to my people is, "I really care about you and the work you're doing," versus, "I'm your boss." I've always found that is what has made somebody or a company successful.

▲

There are a number of things that motivate people. Money, fear, love—all those things. And fear is okay sometimes, but that can't be the main motivator. It's projecting the image that you care about your people.

I had a boss who projected a level of caring that was absolutely amazing. He constantly demonstrated that he acknowledged that we're all in this together, that we're all human beings who have a life other than this.

If he heard somebody was sick he'd call them. When I had a child he brought me and my wife a little gift. He threw parties at his house for us and our spouses, and got people to meet and relax and get to know each other.

As a result, the whole group thought, hey, somebody actually cares about me and what I'm doing. That really makes a difference.

As a result, he got great work out of us.

—*38-year-old Senior Vice President, Sales and Marketing Consumer Product Company*

The Secret of Empowering Reinforcement

The better you expect your people to do, and the more you tell them that, the better they'll do.

▲

The people who you allow the leeway to do the job know that you support them. The ones who know that you think they're going to do well, do great.

And the people you don't have quite the same confidence in, and that you don't give the same leeway and the same support to, don't do as well.

▲

When you're constantly letting people know in some way that you know they're going to do the right thing and do great, and when you let them do it, they often do.

▲

I don't mean to relate the people who work for me to kids, but you hear studies about first- and second- and third-graders, and the kids that are expected to do really well, do. And I think it's almost the same kind of thing. Within some reason.

The people who know I support them, and know I think they're doing a great job, usually do a great job.

**—*39-year-old President*
*International Hotel and Resort Chain***

The Secret of Interpersonal Overexertion

If you're at a disadvantage, you may have to work twice as hard at building relationships.

▲

▲

If you're operating with any perceived "disadvantage"—you're young, or black, or Asian, or a woman, or whatever—you not only have to work twice as hard, you have to work relationships twice as hard. The fact that everything is based on personal relationships is a lesson that it took me a good long while to understand and one which I am still learning and still trying to become better at.

▲

Hard work and workplace results are no guarantee of career success.

I think that the biggest myth in our society is the myth that success comes solely from obtaining the proper credentials and from working hard.

Being black certainly plays a major role in everything that I am able to do. I have noticed that we as African-Americans have bought into a cultural myth. We like to tell everyone that just simply by working hard, you are able to rise to the top.

Well, that has never been true, and when you're talking about institutions and surviving in institutions, that never has been the case.

It's true that working hard gets you into the game, but that alone is not what gets you the biggest prizes offered in the game.

It's the relationships along with the hard work. If you are simply relying upon your hard work and are going to ignore the personal aspect and expect to get the promotion or get the better job, then you are going down the wrong path.

Opinions, especially of African-Americans, are formed extremely quickly in professional situations. If that opinion is a negative one, the die is usually cast, and unless there is a relationship to keep you going, you will not have a long career with that employer.

I've seen that happen to several attorneys who lasted less than a year, because opinions were formed about them very quickly. And they ended up living down to those expectations and leaving the law firm.

In these situations, people always make some mistakes. Because every young attorney makes mistakes. But when the person that you're working for sees you as a younger version of himself, they may overlook the mistakes, because they know they made mistakes themselves.

If, however, you believe that you've gotten there solely on your own merit and are going to sink or swim on your own merit, any mistake shows you don't have the merit. So it's easier for a superior to form the opinion that, since you made this mistake, you just aren't good enough. And then oftentimes you don't get another chance.

It's not just African-Americans; it probably is everyone. White executives who don't focus on relationships probably suffer just as much. If they don't have any personal factors that give them any kind of an advantage, then they probably lose as well. The personal factor can be a golf game or an interest in hockey or whatever. Whatever it is that will give someone a relationship that's beyond just what happens in the office.

▲

Generally, anytime you wander into a situation in which relationships are important and you don't understand that and are simply going to rely on your own wisdom and your own knowledge, you are making a terrible mistake. That is commonly done, and, as a result, careers are lost.

▲

—34-year-old General Counsel
Health and Fitness Company

The Secret of Instantaneous Transmission

Assume that anything negative you say about someone in the organization will get back to them, quickly, and probably in a much worse way than you intended.

▲

There are things that should never be shared with people inside the organization. It's hard to balance that, because if you don't share anything about yourself, then people think you're so cold and machinelike and so perfect that it's hard to warm up to you.

Keep to yourself anything that you might perceive to be a vulnerability about yourself, anything about yourself that could be turned against you.

That also goes for any feelings that you might have about others in the organization, unless it's intentional. Believe me, if I let it out that someone's not in favor, it's planned.

I have learned the mistake of just saying, "Oh, I really don't like that person," and it getting back to them. Or, "This person did something that's really going to screw them up in some sort of way."

▲

It always gets back to them. Always. And usually not in the way you said it, but in some other kind of manifestation that's even worse than what you said. So you really have to be careful about what kinds of things you say, particularly if it involves other people, other people's careers, other people's promotability inside the organization or their positioning inside the organization.

▲

If they're politicking for a specific project to be supported, or something of that nature, and you're opposed to the project, you have to be very careful letting people know where you stand on some of those things. It's very hard.

—38-year-old Senior Vice President
National Retail Store Chain

The Secret of
Intracorporate
Sabotage

Some companies don't behave as teams organized for a common goal, but as loose confederations of warring tribes. Beware of plants, spies, and secret agents.

▲

▲

I have worked in two companies, a small one and a large one, where I worked with people who were "plants." They absolutely were spies.

▲

In one case, it was an individual who worked for me as a subordinate.

I used to always think he was like the idiot son of the Chairman. He was generally pretty incompetent at his particular role. He had never really done that role before. The job was kind of a gift, it seemed.

He screwed up a lot. And he cost the company a lot.

It dawned on me one day when he came to me about a project he'd been working on. It had a $100,000 overrun, which was a significant piece of what the original budget was.

All along we had been having "touch base" sessions every couple of weeks. "How's it going? What's going on with the project? Give me an update."

Never in any of those sessions had he said, "Well, I think I might have a budgetary problem."

Never.

He kept telling me about the progress of the project, and everything was fine.

Well, it finally got to a point where he realized it was out of hand and he came forward and told me about the overrun. I said, "Okay, here's what we're going to do. We're calling the Chief Financial Officer, the Controller, and the Chairman, and we're going to go in and we're going to tell them where we are."

So we went into the meeting. I had already, in advance, called the CFO, called the Controller, to let them know. They were a little appalled, but they said, "It's not going to bankrupt the company, so don't worry about it. But we do need to get it on the table and let the Chairman know where we are."

So we sit down in the meeting and we present all the information.

The Chairman looks over and he says to him, "I think you're doing a yeoman's job. All things considered, with your not having had experience in this area, and the deadlines that you've had to meet . . ." I mean, it was all BS.

He then excuses him from the room.

▲

He then proceeds to rip my face off for about fifteen minutes about how I could have ever let the project get that far out of control.

▲

That's when I realized that it didn't matter what this person did from an accountability standpoint, because he was a protected species in some way. He was literally a plant there to find out what I did in other areas, even though the Chairman had hired me.

That was the kind of plant that I'm talking about. Where somebody has been put into a role specifically to give feedback directly, and is really protected from their own performance.

▲

Many organizations of that type are little fiefdoms, and every-one has their little moat that they build around their little kingdom.

▲

They would try to kill each other. I used to go to meetings where guys would wear hats with shark fins on them. I'm not kidding. At social kinds of things like company picnics the guys would wear shark fins.

When I first got there, I wondered, what is all that about?

Then I figured it out.

It was a shark pond.

—38-year-old Senior Vice President
National Retail Store Chain

The Secret of
Subtle Entrapment

When you step into a new situation, realize that you need to get the lay of the land before you act.

▲

▲

If you are brought into an organization and you have a reputation for being a high flyer or a star moving up, there are situations where people are trying to set you up for failure. It can be done in a variety of ways.

▲

One way that I've experienced is when someone gives you a job and doesn't tell you what you need to know to do the job, and allows you to flounder around to find out what you need to know. Then later they can say, "You should have known that."

Another trap is, because you feel the need to prove yourself, there is a tendency to act for effect too early, before you see the traps. The lesson I've learned from a couple of such experiences is that, as hard as it is to do, when I go into a new position I purposely lay low for at least three months.

I lay low in the sense of not making any dramatic moves, not making any pronouncements. I'll do the job, but I'm basically in a listening and learning mode for at least ninety days until I figure out where people are and where the traps are.

There may be a lot of pressure, sometimes from people setting the traps, to get you to make a move. But I have found that the smartest thing to do is to resist at all costs, until you understand the lay of the land.

Not long ago I came into a new unit, and it turned out that the person I had replaced was kind of floating and was very interested in having me fail, because he clearly had a lot of pain and disappointment about being replaced.

The setup was that he was still in a position to look over my shoulder. In this case I laid low for six months. The trap was that he had done many things that were wrong for the job, which is why he had been removed.

On the other hand, he was close enough to the job that he was putting me under constant pressure to do certain things.

Nobody was up-front enough with me to tell me what was going on.

I just had to figure out that here was this guy giving me lots of advice in a supposedly supportive way and everything he was telling me to do was the wrong thing to do.

This individual who was my superior was definitely trying to give me the wrong advice or steer me in the wrong direction. And that continued for two years until he retired and I got his job. That was a very open enmity.

▲

I decided that this guy really had set his sights on destroying my career! Once I figured that out, I made up my mind that he was going to go before I did. That was a case in which I actively worked to protect myself. I consciously never stooped to his level of tactics, but I made sure that people understood what tactics he was using.

▲

I made the difference in our behavior visible enough for people to see. I never brought up the subject, but when people brought it up, I was candid with them.

I didn't want to give people the impression I was fanning the flames, but when people asked me a question, they were going to get a direct answer. And in the end, as frequently happens, he self-destructed.

His behavior was so flagrant and so irrational and so clearly based on his own insecurity that whatever talent he brought to the job, he was just not productive.

He hoisted himself on his own petard.

▲

If you give people like that enough rope, they'll generally hang themselves. I did not actively subvert him. I think that would have backfired. I was selectively candid and I selectively sought advice. And in the course of seeking advice from friends, they clearly got a picture of what was happening.

▲

—37-year-old Vice President
Global Telecommunications Company

78

The Secret of Universal Discretion

You can't always trust everyone in the organization.

▲

One lesson I learned is: Don't necessarily trust anybody, okay?

For example, don't talk about your boss if you don't like your boss.

Don't say anything bad to anybody, even if it's your best friend and you trust them, and you think they'll never say a thing. You never know.

They may not tell your boss that you said what you said, but they may tell somebody else who may tell somebody else, and then somebody else, and eventually the boss will find out.

▲

Just don't ever bad-mouth your boss, your client, or whomever to anybody, because it can get back.

▲

I did a very stupid thing once. I bad-mouthed my boss to my boss's boss.

The new head of the department was taking all of the junior people out to lunch to get acquainted, to ask, "How're you doing? What do you like? Who don't you like? How's your job going?"

So she takes me out to lunch to give me my review and tell me what they think of me, and for me to say how am I feeling because the morale in the department was low.

So I spent five, ten, fifteen minutes talking about, "This is great and this is great and this is great, but I have my one frustration—my immediate boss. He's very smart and very lazy: comes in to work at 11:00, leaves at 4:00. Really sharp, but does no work."

So in a very nice, diplomatic way I told her about him, and I had been told that my peers who felt the same way were going to be telling her the same thing. It turned out they didn't. They chickened out. So I told her.

▲

It turns out she was sleeping with him. I guess, in the end, you've just got to be careful.

▲

Watch what you say to other people; don't always trust other people. Don't talk in elevators.

I was once standing with a friend of mine in his office, my back was to the door, and I made a comment about my boss; "He's such an asshole."

And he walked in, and he knew I was talking about him. I didn't use his name, but he knew I was talking about him, okay? I had left a meeting with him in which we had disagreed. When I looked up, I turned red and he knew I was talking about him.

▲

I was supposed to become a vice president that year, and I didn't, and I think it was because I pissed him off so much.

▲

—34-year-old President
Advertising Agency

The Secret of
Radical Neutrality

If your company gets mired in factional disputes, try to resist choosing sides, and stay focused on doing the job.

▲

▲

If your company is embroiled in some kind of factional dispute, it's probably better to try to remain neutral than to cast your lot with one side or the other, regardless of who looks like they're going to win, because not only might you pick the wrong side, but you may take your eye off the day-to-day operational ball.

▲

Once, our company went through an internal struggle between two factions.

It came to the point where if you found yourself aligned politically with the wrong side you could quickly be out of a job, even though you might have been a valuable employee.

One of the cofounders said, "Well, you've got to decide what side of the fence you want to be on." My response was, "I didn't know there was supposed to be a fence."

So you had both factions going in different directions. When the cofounder walked down the hallway, the president would look at me and roll his eyes.

It made my life very difficult because I was new to the upper-management level, and one faction was trying to pull me while the other tried to win me over.

At the time all my consideration was to continue working with the middle managers, who really weren't "factioned" in such a sense, to try to keep things rolling from a day-to-day operational standpoint.

I kept a lot of my relationships and day-to-day efforts focused on, okay, let's look at sales coming in, let's look at getting orders installed and servicing customers and just keep things going while the rest of this stuff runs its course. Somebody's got to keep the company rolling, and that was what middle management was trying to do.

That's the key point of it, networking with everyone, having a number of individuals who recognize your abilities, and not relying on one individual.

▲

Nobody can lay blame on somebody who is trying to focus on what the job is—keeping the product, the company, the operational aspects moving. If you're an individual who can display a high degree of integrity and honesty, and your views are respected and acknowledged by your peers or other executive management that you may report to, I think ultimately they can't fault you for not taking a side.

▲

—34-year-old Vice President, Client Services
Information Systems Company

The Secret of Selective Battle Management

The fewer turf battles you pick, the more chance you have of winning the ones you do pick.

▲

▲

There are fiefdoms and turf in all organizations, and you're always juggling between those things to produce your deals and revenues, but you have to understand how to pick your battles.

▲

There will be times when you're going to have to fight for certain issues within your organization, and other times when you really don't have to be confrontational.

That includes your employees.

There are certain times I want to be extremely critical and harsh because they just didn't do what they were supposed to do at the level that was necessary, but I'll decide to instead be more conciliatory (i.e., use more finesse) to enable the employee to recognize that maybe their work product wasn't up to the required level, or that their approach wasn't the right way to go.

I'm not a confrontational manager. I try to be a little bit more charismatic. Picking your battles is a philosophy of mine. Selective battle management.

You can't go with the club all the time.

You don't always have to exert the maximum force. You can't just always run around with your club and try to beat people up because they may be infringing on your turf. There are different ways of dealing with it. There are times to concede and there are times when you dig in.

The less you pull out your club, the more weight it will carry when you do.

People who tend to be confrontational all the time eventually get rejected by people. They say, "I don't want to deal with him. He's an asshole." And that cripples their effectiveness within the organization. I equate that to managing up, managing down, managing across, and managing turf.

▲

If you see a turf issue coming toward you, you should stop and ask yourself, "Is this worth drawing a line in the sand and going to war over?"

▲

—40-year-old Managing Partner
Investment Bank

The Secret of
Strategic Altruism

The people you turn around can become your most powerful allies.

▲

A lot of situations can turn out positively; for example, taking someone who may have wronged you and turning him or her into an ally. I think it's normal; it can happen on a weekly or a monthly basis because people don't trust you unless they really know you.

People have first impressions of you—and if you are moving quickly they're going to be twice as skeptical. So they may do something to you before they even know you just as a reaction.

But what you do is educate afterward, and even in a situation that they may be involved with peripherally, you do something that helps them. And all of a sudden, they come around and say, "You know, I was wrong."

▲

Those are extremely valuable allies, the ones you turn around.

▲

The other situation is that there are just some who are never going to get it, but the fact is that you're going to move beyond them, and so their power's not going to be in your way for more than a moment in time. So it's really not worth it. Don't lash out, because that could blow you down or delay you or cause a problem.

People have a view of you. It happens in any work environment. But they already have pre-judgments of the kind of person you are, and maybe what your potential is, and maybe what your weaknesses are. What they do is based on those impressions, and they treat you that way.

You almost have to actively try to rid them of those things over time.

You do that by actually helping them in an unselfish way, which surprises the hell out of them. Once you do that, it sort of opens the door and they say, "God, I was wrong about you. I knew you were good at this or that, but I never expected . . ."

I think anybody who is good at what he or she does constantly faces this. The first thing you're going to do with most people is knock them off balance.

▲

Although they'll respect you for what you do well, they'll always try to figure out something that you don't do well, or assume that you're this or that in a negative way. That's their own insecurities at work.

▲

And the minute that you actually help those people and show that, even though you might have those negatives they shouldn't be worried about it, you can turn them around.

—36-year-old Executive Vice President
Hollywood Talent Agency

The Secret of Empathetic Brutality

If you have to fire someone, an aggressive display of compassion can pay dividends in the long run.

▲

▲

In my career what I've learned that's been most important are people skills.

▲

I've learned how one can be aggressive and get others to do what is necessary in a manner that is constructive and preserves relationships. Every person is different and must be communicated with and dealt with in a different manner.

▲

I attribute much of my success to people skills—the ability to deal straightforwardly, honestly, and effectively with people. And not to burn bridges along the way.

▲

I can remember being in a situation with a film director a week or two before a film was to commence production. Because of my own realization that this particular individual was unprepared for the task ahead, I had to call him in and fire him literally a week before the picture was to commence shooting.

I'd say I handled it successfully, first, because it was the right business decision to make. And, second, because this individual is still a friend with whom I have continued to do business.

▲

Part of what I do and part of what any manager does, is that you often spend a large part of your day having to say no, and delivering bad news.

▲

In the film business, maybe 200, 250 projects are submitted to a studio every year. The studio's only going to make ten or fifteen of those projects, so you're always saying no.

▲

It's how one says no and how one delivers bad news that is also the sign of a good executive and good manager.

▲

Here we're talking about the firing of an individual, which obviously has potentially grave consequences for one's career and livelihood.

When that kind of news needs to be delivered, there are a couple of rules. Number one, you always deliver the news in person, if you can. Never over the phone.

Number two, you always deliver that news alone in a room; you don't have colleagues or friends around. You deliver the news one on one, eyeball to eyeball. That's the most effective method, because there are things that can be said between two people that often are not said when there are three, four, or more people in the room.

So those are the first two rules, and this instance was no exception. I had the fellow come in and we sat down, and basically I was firm and to the point. Essentially I said this is not going to work; I'm afraid you're not going to be able to direct the picture. Then I explained the reason why. Don't let someone squirm. This way you can deal with the emotional impact, as opposed to going through twenty minutes of "Look, things aren't working," etc.

This was an individual who didn't want to let go of it for a long time, so there were many subsequent phone calls, including phone calls from his wife late at night.

It really took a couple of days and many hours with the director and his wife to effect the break. However devastating it was at the moment, I think it was handled in the manner that was in the best interests of the film. But I still preserved the relationship with a director who I think is very talented.

Handling the dismissal this way allowed him to do further work on other projects, under other circumstances that were better suited to his strengths and talents. So I guess to that extent all goals were accomplished.

—35-year-old President
Motion Picture Studio

The Secret of Intellectual Egalitarianism

Don't be intimidated by anyone. There's a good chance you're at least as smart as they are.

▲

▲

One of the biggest surprises in my career was when I figured out that business is not always full of the brightest people.

▲

Many of the people who rise to the top of their intellectual or creative powers become doctors or scientists or artists.

Business is not always blessed with the most blinding people in terms of intellect or creativity or the power to do something.

▲

If you have reasonable intelligence, the ability to work hard and create something on your own, the ability to lead, the ability to listen, and if you have a good set of values, you will do well.

▲

It just blows me away how easy it is for people with just those simple, basic traits to do extremely well.

A lot of things are pretty commonsensical. I haven't used my high school calculus in a long time, but I do use my street savvy every minute.

Sometimes I think people think that they have to be Superman or Superwoman to do well.

The fact is that there are not a lot of Einsteins running around in management.

—39-year-old Senior Vice President
Consumer Packaged Goods

The Secret of Shared Vulnerability

Acknowledging that you're not perfect can help you build relationships. The more trust and empathy you build, the more successful you'll be.

▲

I can be very aggressive, and I can be very competitive, and I can also be very empathic. As a gay man, I have one foot in the "dominant culture" and another foot outside it.

▲

You have to be willing to be vulnerable. I've had to really encourage my people to be willing to be vulnerable with me. I say, "Look, I'm not here to do your job for you, I'm here to help you with your development and with your tasks."

▲

"When you're feeling uncomfortable, whether you're stressed out or unsure about what to do, or whatever, I want you to come in and tell me. I'm not going to think badly of you because of that. I'm going to say, okay, let's talk about how I can help you."

So my people have been able to do that, and some amazingly positive things have happened.

I think they become much better leaders as a result of that.

Over time, my business relationships have become much more trusting.

You have to have an environment where you trust people and where you feel that they trust you.

I wouldn't stay very long in an environment where I didn't have that trust. Life's too short.

—38-year-old Vice President
High Technology Manufacturing

The Secret of
Multicultural
Enlightenment

Understanding cultural diversity will give
you a competitive advantage.

▲

     This is the first time I've been a minority for my skin color in a work environment.

I'm white. And in a black company.

▲

This is going to become more and more of an issue as you look at the demographics and the fact that blacks, Hispanics, and Asians together will be approaching 40 percent of the population by the year 2010. Everybody's got to know the feeling of what it's like to walk in and be automatically different just because of your skin color—whether it's being resented, or people feeling sorry for you or good for you or

nervous about you or threatened or whatever. You have to know how to cut through that stuff.

▲

You have to learn how to cut through it and get to what you need in order to get your business going, and how different approaches and different strategies are called for in different sorts of ethnic environments.

The best time to instill that is at a young age because they don't give a shit at that point what color you are. Nobody has any pretensions. If you grow up with it being natural, I think you're in good shape.

It's kind of hard to do it once you're already grown up, but don't shy away from ethnic diversity.

Learn how to use it to your advantage, which doesn't mean exploiting other races, but understanding them.

Understand the issues and understand the techniques to get color dropped as an issue as quickly as possible in a negotiating situation.

Get as much exposure as you can communicating with other ethnic groups.

As much as possible, look at it as an opportunity so that you understand where they're coming from and how they react, because there are very subtle little things that allow you to either get something done or have something blow up.

▲

I've found the things that make you uncomfortable are the situations you learn the most from.

▲

—34-year old Chief Financial Officer
Broadcasting Company

PROJECTS AND PROPOSALS

DECISIONS

COMMUNICATIONS

The Secret of Incremental Progress

Handling the little things can be more important than hitting the home runs.

▲

▲

The best boss I ever had taught me that I should look for "incremental progress."

▲

I think a mistake that people make, and that I have made as well, is thinking that they "deserve" a promotion.

"I deserve to be promoted; when's it going to happen?" It doesn't usually happen that way; you can't demand it or feel entitled to it. It doesn't come that way.

Frequently you try to hit a "home run" to get recognition.

And you can do that, it happens, but not as frequently as if you keep hitting singles and get around the bases.

▲

Go for the incremental progress and don't get discouraged by

knowing that you've got this goal and you're just chipping away at it.

▲

I remember when I was coming up in this business line. In my opinion, I had hit a home run. I got a new business up and started, and it was doing great. And so I thought, "Where's my reward?" It didn't happen, and I was frustrated.

So then, of course, I'm out there looking for the next home run, and it's eluding me. I'm getting very frustrated because I can't get it. When I actually changed jobs, I stopped looking at it that way, and I started saying, "Okay, this is something that really needs to be done, and I can add some value here," and I did it.

When I was trying to constantly hit home runs, I was alienating people all over the place.

I was being downright pushy about it. I might have been right, but people really don't want to be pushed around all the time.

Sometimes you've got to give other people time to come around on things.

▲

I was coached to take the path of incremental progress. I started getting more and more people to be part of the process; I did more consensus building. And then instead of hitting the home run, I got there, but with a lot fewer bodies lying around and a lot less animosity toward me.

▲

Keep going for the singles.

You can get on the scoreboard both ways: by loading up the bases and driving a guy home, or by knocking it out of the park.

And if you strike out a lot going for home runs, your batting average looks pretty terrible.

—37-year-old Senior Vice President
Financial Institution

The Secret of
Fearless Initiative

If you're not getting burned regularly,
you're not trying hard enough.

▲

The big surprise for me with career success is that there's no trick
to it. It's not who has the MBA, it's not who's the smartest.

It's who has the brass balls, whatever you want to call it, to
just be on top of it, work hard, work smart, and then actually do
something.

Knowledge isn't what's valuable; it's what you do with it.

It's having the guts to just go out and do something, make a
decision, act on it.

Too many people sit around and wait. They're not sure if it's the
right thing to do. They're afraid to take a stand.

Think it out, then do something. Don't wait too long. Use your
gut and then just kind of stick with it—and be flexible, though.

I've never really been afraid to go out there and be different or to come to the front of the pack and say, "Hey, let's go this way."

▲

It's not that complex or complicated. Only one-tenth of 1 percent of the human population is actually willing to take the lead on anything. And therefore those who are at least get the opportunity.

▲

Most people want to be led. They're followers, and the one-tenth of 1 percent who are willing to jump on top of the heap and just kind of say, "I think it's this way" are the ones who really make it. And that was interesting to me, because I thought, "I'm not an engineer, I'm not a lawyer, I'm not a doctor. I don't have an MBA."

You can't just learn by watching. You have to learn by getting burned, too. Because if you're not burning, guess what? You're not going to the wall.

▲

If you're not burning yourself and learning by your own screw-ups, you're not going to the wall enough.

▲

Use what you have. That's really the difference between knowledge and power probably. A lot of people have knowledge; using it is power. That's the key.

Risk and hard decisions can be painful, but sometimes the biggest reward can emerge from the most painful situation.

No pain, no gain—you've heard that a million times.

When you go out on a limb, there's always some pain, there's always a lot of risk. And then the reward is kind of proportionate. And I get a kick out of that. I hate being second; I hate losing more than I like to win.

▲

I know smarter people, better-looking people. I know people who are probably even better with people than I am. But you

can really clear out the room when you say, "Now, all right, I think we should do this, and here's why." Put your butt on the line.

▲

—*32-year-old Executive Vice President*
Computer Software Company

The Secret of
Downside Thinking

The more you ask, "What can go wrong?" the better off you'll be.

▲

▲

One distinguishing factor which has made me valuable is being a good "downside thinker." Instead of thinking of all the things that can go right, I try to think of all the things that can go wrong.

▲

I tend to be very careful and do a lot of homework on people. I generally assume that people mean well, but I always consider that some people may be out to hurt you or have a different agenda.

You have to guard against being too negative, or else you won't end up doing anything. However, I look at a situation and try not to think of all the great things that can happen to me. I go home at night and think about all the bad things that can happen to me, and all the things that I missed. The next day I usually come in to work a lot smarter.

It's important to have the discipline to look at a problem and say, "What are the ten things that can go wrong?" Once you've thought of things that can go wrong, then you often can insure that not as many of those things go wrong or you can plan for them.

Sometimes people don't like to hear about the flaws in a transaction. It takes courage to stand in the crowd and say, "Here are the items that I'm really concerned about."

One of the things I've learned is to keep a lot of "powder dry" or to keep a lot of capital available. Generally, all investment and business situations move through positive and negative cycles, and it's important to recognize that you can rarely buy at the bottom and sell at the top. All the money is made in between. So it's always good to keep some capital available as the cycle changes.

For example, prior to being involved in a health-care company, our investment partnership was fully invested (but not leveraged) in the stock market crash of 1987. Because I always believe that something can go wrong, we were greatly hedged, turning a negative situation into a real positive.

If you develop the discipline to think of the ten logical risk factors for every situation and plan accordingly, you have a significant ingredient for success.

Try and take things apart and look at them from as many sides as you can think of and then if the idea still has merit, push ahead!

—*32-year-old Senior Vice President and Treasurer*
Health Care Service Provider

The Secret of Institutional Digestibility

Don't overcook an idea before you present it. Give others a chance to help improve and "own" it.

▲

You can't see things as only one way.

▲

If you're sure you know the right answer, right away that should be suspect because there are always three or four different ways of getting to a solution. If you think you have the right answer, you have to carefully study your organization first, because you might not have come up with a solution the organization can "digest."

▲

Get your idea translated into digestible form.

When you come in with a good idea or solution and your boss changes it, don't take that as a criticism.

The boss needs to feel like he's added something.

▲

Your idea could have been perfect when it walked in the door, but a lot of bosses are insecure. If he doesn't think, "Well, I have something to add here," then he figures, "Why do they need me?" You have to be able to say to your bosses and colleagues: "Thank you for improving my solution."

▲

—39-year-old President
Consumer Products Company

The Secret of Exponential Overdelivery

Don't just perform the task. Try to leverage the result.

▲

▲

When you're asked to do work for a superior, the real trick is to learn that person so that not only do you complete the task that they've asked you to do, but you go one step beyond to deliver added value.

▲

You begin to think like them, so you anticipate what they're going to ask you to do.

That's tricky, because a lot of times people get their wings clipped because they were asked to go to step 3 and they went to step 5 and got a negative reaction, like, "Who do you think you are? You're not running this. I asked you to go to step 3 and just do step 3." You've got to understand that.

But there are times when you know you've got to get some

progression beyond what you're doing. Time is of the essence. The person you're working for is trying to be leveraged by your activities.

If you do it, and you come in and say, "Well, I completed these three tasks, and, oh, by the way, I've begun to think about 4 and 5," the person may say, "Great, wonderful." Well, that's leveraging that person, showing this person that you thoroughly understand what you're doing. That's showing initiative.

In this organization that's key. My sense is that those things are key in any work environment.

But that is very key here, because we are looking to be leveraged by the people below us so we can do more deals. Your boss doesn't necessarily want you to do the task, period; he or she wants you to leverage the results.

But there are situations where you have to understand that maybe you're over your head, you don't understand, you're not going to understand despite the fact that you're confident that you do.

▲

You have to be in tune with the people you're working with.

▲

—40-year-old Managing Partner
Investment Bank

The Secret of Megatrend Micromanagement

Find a major "hot button" issue for your company and tackle it.

▲

▲

There are opportunities or problems that are clearly of utmost importance to senior management, even though they're not necessarily the stated objective.

▲

If you can come up with an innovative program or strategy that can have results for those areas, it can make all the difference in the world.

I think that you can find the areas that are most important if you really learn to read between the lines and listen well to not just the words that people say, but how they say them, the things they get excited about when they're talking, the things they have a tendency to repeat.

When I was a product manager we were doing a project on what started out as a revamping of the guest comment system. People had probably revamped it a million times over the years.

By taking that project and changing the slant of it, tying it into the company's overall quality program, which was something that was an absolute hot button to the president at the time, I did something that became a very crucial turning point at the company.

It was an issue that was really a small issue, but I took the slant that was really important to senior management.

—39-year-old President
International Hotel and Resort Chain

The Secret of Opportunistic Masochism

Don't automatically reject a "lousy assignment." It could be a career maker.

▲

▲

Don't be afraid of a "crummy assignment." The worst that will happen is that you'll fail, and that might be understood if it were truly that crummy. Whereas if you make it work, or you at least impress people on the way, that's a big win, isn't it?

▲

I have someone on my staff now to whom I gave a lousy and very difficult assignment. I'd given him no staff with which to do it.

He has impressed not only me, but probably three or four other people in the company, not only with how well he is doing this very difficult job, but also with how happily he is doing it, with the good will he's built with people inside and outside of the company. He has made something happen where a lot of other people would have just thrown up their hands in frustration.

When the right opportunity presents itself, his name will be on the top of two or three people's lists as somebody to pick, because he's been very impressive in this very difficult situation.

He didn't ask, "Why me? Boy, did I get the crummy assignment. So and so has ten people working for him and I don't have anybody. How does that look? This is terrible." Instead he's done it beautifully and cheerfully and substantively, and without a lot of direction.

He's very self-motivated. I think that attitude is very important.

There is frequently a herd instinct. When something seems like the hot area, everybody wants to get into it. That's when many people will be fighting for a few good jobs. And, yes, if you're one of the ones picked, what a great feeling it might be and a great opportunity it might be.

Everybody wants to get into it. Also, when something looks good, that's when the business competition is going to get tough, also.

▲

Finding opportunity often is finding something that looks tough to do, and taking it on when other people aren't that interested in taking it on.

▲

When I went over to strategic planning, people thought I was a little nuts.

It was a small department that had never contributed anything to the company before. The area I was leaving was hot and rolling. People were dying to get into it, and I walked out, I left it.

It wasn't that I was so smart, but in retrospect it was a smart thing. It's what distinguished me. When we succeeded in doing something, people started saying, "Hmm, that's an interesting area."

I tried to hire three people to work for me. I tried to pick good people from inside the company. Not one of them came to work for me because of what they thought they were leaving. Why should they leave a hot, sexy area to work in a not-so-hot area?

Against my own wishes, I was forced to do all my hiring from outside the company. I ran ads and I hired. I found three terrific people. They've done great things. They have done well, and they are now very close to being promoted.

Now the same people I tried to hire are saying, "It is so unfair. All the new people get the good assignments and get promoted." I'm thinking, "Wait a minute. I tried to hire you; where were you? You didn't want to take the risk, or what seemed to you to be the risk."

I'm not saying you should do something foolish, but this is why they call it work. Sometimes it is hard!

—37-year-old Senior Vice President
Financial Institution

The Secret of Executional Paranoia

The last 5 percent of detail can separate the heroes from the losers.

▲

▲

I believe the battles are won and lost in the last 5 percent of detail. Everybody gets the first 80 percent. Most people get the first 95 percent. What makes the difference is people who get that last 5 percent.

▲

Whatever it is the client comes up with, you've already done it, you've already taken care of it. You've dotted every "i," crossed every "t."

Everything flows smoothly. There aren't any dropped balls. You're not late to the meeting because you came in that morning and the copy machine was broken. Why did you wait until the morning of the meeting? You could have done it the night before. It doesn't matter how late it was. That's attention to detail.

While people don't even notice that you're caring about each detail, the overall impression it creates is superior. Like, if a guy gets a hair cut every couple of weeks, you never even notice that he's gotten one, versus letting it get too long and then getting it cut.

That's the way attention to detail is. The presence of it should be unnoticed.

We were to make a presentation on short notice to a large banking client on the East Coast, and the staff had done a very nice job of the analysis. The meeting was the next morning, I was reviewing the presentation one last time, and it was evening already.

In looking through the final draft, I noticed that each of the pages was just a little bit different—the software had scaled each of the graphs just a bit differently. It made it difficult to compare one chart to the next as one turned the pages.

I'm sure the staff kind of groaned when I had them manually adjust the scales on each page to make them visually comparable. It didn't change the data, but it did eliminate just one more potential for problems the next day.

There are two kinds of staff members in this situation. The one type rolls their eyes and thinks, "What a neurotic bitch."

The other type thinks, "Hey, I learned something tonight."

After the changes were made, we walked through it one last time, verbally this time, as if we were presenting it to the client. At one point in the presentation I found that I had to flip back to a graph several pages earlier for reference. I said, "I know everything is properly page numbered and ready to be bound, but we really have to repeat this graph here."

So, the conclusion of the story is that the next day at the presentation the client happened to compliment us on two or three things that, coincidentally, we had changed the night before. Then, when he got to the point in the presentation where we had decided to repeat the chart, he started to flip back to the earlier page and we said, "No, just flip the page," and, finding the necessary chart, he said, "Oh, I see that, as always, you are one step ahead of me."

That's what I mean about that last 5 percent. I'm not saying that without it the meeting would not have gone well, but it made a difference in the overall impression we left with the client.

Was it worth it? I think so. In fact, I would submit that it's that last 5 percent that separates out from among all the bright ones those who are going to rise above all the others.

It's not that they're smarter; it may not be that they work harder. It's just that they have that capacity for those last percentage points of detail.

▲

I worry about 100 things my client doesn't know I worry about, eighty of which they would probably think I was wasting my time on, but I can't tell which twenty they are going to appreciate, so I worry about all 100, so that the twenty are always covered. It creates a sense of confidence that everything will be taken care of.

▲

—38-year-old Partner
Management Consulting Firm

The Secret of Pragmatic Resignation

There are some things you can't
influence. Don't agonize over them.

▲

I don't worry about things that are out of my goddamn control.

I had a sales manager who once told me to take care of the little things, that the big things will take care of themselves. And I never forgot that.

What he really meant was that if you're taking care of the stuff day in and day out, all the things you need to take care of, the big deals will hit. You'll get your breaks.

▲

Take care of those things day to day. When you say you're going to do something, do it. You say you're going to make a phone call, make the phone call. Good or bad, pain or pleasure, do it. The little things basically will get you the big ones.

▲

And what ties in nicely with that is a little philosophy I call the mirror syndrome.

▲

It basically means that you've got to be willing to look in the mirror every night and say, "Did I do what I thought I was going to do today? Did I give it the full effort today? Did I go to the wall today?"

▲

And it's funny, every day, with very minor exceptions, I know I can look in the mirror and say, "Yeah, I did."

I did all the little things every day. So I'm going to get the big things. And if I don't, you know what? Screw it. It was out of my control.

I like to be in control in the sense that I have a lot of faith in my own abilities and capabilities. If I have more things in control than out of my control, I think I'm going to be successful.

But don't worry about the stuff you can't control. Handle the things that you can.

This company has been a zoo.

We've gone from a basement to $75,000,000 in four years.

You have to keep cranking and keep going, and people ask, "How do you have the energy? How do you not burn out? How come you don't have any ulcers? I never see you take an aspirin."

I handle things that I'm in control of. I do the little things every day. I check the mirror at night, and I've got nothing to worry about, win, lose, or draw.

I've got thirty-two salespeople, and my job's to generate revenue. If I don't do it, I'm gone; if I do do it, great. I'm a hero or I'm a dog on a quarterly basis. Thankfully every quarter I've been a hero.

Sometimes my sales reps get down on themselves because we push hard every month, every quarter. We want the deals, and we don't always get them. You should be hard on yourself, but not to the point where it affects your business.

There are always going to be last-minute hitches. Somebody got hit by a truck; somebody had a re-org. The purchasing agent put it on the bottom of the pile instead of the top of the pile—whatever.

And what I'll do a lot of the time is say, "Look, did you handle all the things that you were in control of? Getting them the contract when you said you would? Doing a demo when you said you would? Getting the guy to answer their questions on the phone when you said you would? All those things that you control in the sales cycle—did you do all them to a 't'?" "Yeah." All right.

"What happened here? Why is it going to defer?" "Well, Jimmy Jo Bob went to Germany because the data center there has blown up and he won't be back until next Friday."

I'll say, "That's out of your control. Don't worry about it. You make sure that when he gets back, everything's ready. That's your job. Because if he comes back and you've been dorking around or not staying on top of it, and things aren't perfectly ready for him, then you made a mistake. Otherwise you haven't."

▲

Worry about and handle the things in your control. Then 80 percent of the time, you get what you want when you want. The other 20 percent of the time, guess what? You can't control it anyway.

▲

At least you can look in the mirror and say, "Hey, look, I did everything I could. I gave it the best shot I could."

—32-year-old Executive Vice President
Computer Software Company

The Secret of Competitive Candor

Don't be afraid to deliver a well-reasoned point of view. Even if it's killed, it may boost your reputation.

▲

Sooner or later in their careers most people will face a situation where a decision needs to be made, and those involved in the decision-making process will dance around the issue until they get an idea of how the majority of the group feels.

For managers, such occurrences take place almost on a daily basis. If you are expected to be part of a group that is in a policy- or decision-making capacity for your organization, then you had better be well versed on those issues affecting the business.

▲

If you have researched the specific issue and you've developed a point of view based on facts, then state your case and support it.

▲

Don't dance around waiting for the "majority flow." Come forth and state your position in a professional fashion and back it up. At the same time, be receptive to what others in the group are saying. You don't want to be perceived as stubborn.

▲

When I say back it up, I mean go the extra mile—which surprisingly many managers don't do—and research the hell out of the issue. Get the facts: competitive scenarios, market penetration, market forecasts, etc.

▲

In most organizations once an individual reaches the level of management, it becomes extremely competitive. Many people, particularly ex-athletes, thrive on this competition and are very successful because they understand the concept of preparation and training before the big game.

If you can put forth a point of view when others are showing uncertainty and indecisiveness, you will be the first to be asked to explain it. If you have done your homework and have supporting research and facts that substantiate your position, a great level of credibility comes with that.

Without a doubt, that separates someone from the pack.

I recall an incident when a decision was being made by my company that I did not agree with. I set up a management meeting to discuss and review what I felt were the dangers of such a move. The decision was nevertheless approved and implemented.

Seven months later a meeting was called to evaluate the decision's impact. What came out of that meeting was best stated by our CEO when he said, "Hey, guys, we screwed up. We never should have done that. Somebody said so seven months ago. Let's ax it; let's end it."

There was enormous satisfaction on my part because seven months earlier I had been the "somebody" who, with supporting research data, had stated and held my position against it. Sometimes you're right, and sometimes you're wrong. In this case, I was right.

▲

DON'T BE AFRAID OF STATING YOUR POINT OF VIEW.

▲

The bottom line is that if you have the backup, if you've done your homework and present the issues in an objective and professional manner, even if they don't agree with you, you will gain your peers' and superiors' respect because you have dedicated time and effort to justifying it for the betterment of the organization.

In most cases, even if you "lose" your position on the issue, you may come away defeated but with much more credibility than those who were the "winners."

▲

Keep in mind that "defeat" can be a relative term and that the calendar may prove it to be very short-lived.

▲

In this case, defeat lasted only seven months, after which came "victory."

—35-year-old Senior Vice President, Marketing
Health Care Provider

The Secret of Tenacious Advocacy

If you believe strongly in a project, don't give up on it too easily.

▲

If you think you've got something really great and somebody shoots it down, don't give it up.

Don't roll over.

Defend it, and keep selling it.

▲

Don't be obnoxious, but if you really believe in something, and you think it's right, then sell it hard and defend it—don't roll over.

▲

But also know the person that you're selling it to.

I once was trying to get a client to buy a particular advertising campaign.

I knew that this guy's boss would love that advertising. This guy was very concerned about what his boss thought of him, and in our presentations it was clear to me that he didn't see in the campaign what it was that his boss was going to fall in love with.

I had to find the right way of bringing it up, but not by saying, "Hey, Joe, your boss is going to love this!" I took him out to lunch and subtly steered him in that direction, and I knew when it finally hit him. He opened his eyes and was thinking, "Yeah, my boss is going to like this. He'll love it."

You push the button by leading them to it.

I did have the benefit of having worked on that business for a few years, so I knew his boss, and I knew who the different players were. So I could steer it. But know who you're selling to and then don't give up; just keep selling.

▲

I think there are three parts to selling something. There's the pre-sell, then there's the actual sell, and then there's the post-sell.

▲

The actual sell is that big meeting with twenty people, where it's very hard for someone to say, "I love that." In that last example I didn't have the chance to do the pre-sell.

For the pre-sell, I'm not saying you sit there and explain everything he's going to see, but I could have had a session with him the day before, saying, "You're going to see a dozen things. Six are great. Three of them you should move ahead to test tomorrow, but there's one that I've got to tell you is going to drive this business through the roof." And then I'll talk conceptually about it.

Then the next day when you get into the meeting with twenty people, you can kind of let him know which one you thought was that grand slam. Then after the meeting, you do the post-sell, and that's the best way to make it work.

It just never works to walk into a conference room with somebody who's a decision maker, and expect them to look at a whole bunch of work with twenty people around and then make a decision. It just never works that way.

You've got to keep selling afterward because people fall out of love with things, too, and then they get nervous.

—34-year-old President
Advertising Agency

The Secret of Multilateral Thinking

Constantly push your thinking and actions into more global contexts.

▲

▲

When I look at the people I think are the superstars, whether they're working for me or for someone else, it's the ones who think beyond the box.

▲

For example, I have someone who doesn't report to me directly but is in a department that reports to me.

I went to her awhile ago with a very short message, saying, "We need a status update on the following. Would you please hit these three projects in this area." She went away.

Then she called me back and said, "Well, what about projects four and five, which I also know fit in those areas but you didn't ask me to do the update on."

The reason I didn't ask her was because I didn't think she had the information, and I was going to do it myself. She said, "Just tell me who I should get in touch with to get that information."

She was trying to figure out what my intent was. Not just saying, "Okay, she asked me to do these three, and I'll go do them well."

Instead she was saying, "Well, gee, if she wants these three, she probably wants these additional two as well. Let's just expand it so that it's complete." This particular individual works that way all the time.

She's constantly pushing the thinking and saying, "Have you thought about this? Or should we be doing this as well?" Or she'll call me up and say, "Do you want me to take the lead on doing such and such, so and so?" And that goes a really long way.

In general, for people who are running departments, there's so much to do. My feeling is that if I can find people who want to take on the additional responsibility, good for them.

I'll give them all the support they need.

How much can someone screw up on something anyhow?

There are few decisions that anyone who reports to me could make that would destroy this company. In fact, I can't think of any.

You just hope that they don't commit the really big blunder that gets you into trouble!

I take great personal pride and a certain amount of credit for anything accomplished by anyone who works for me.

Not that I'm taking credit away from them, but if they did it, that only reflects well on me. If they did well, it reflects well on me.

▲

You have to think beyond the obvious to ask, "What are the implications, what are the repercussions? Are we looking at the right issues?" I think you can do that every single day.

▲

Think about not just doing the tasks, but also, "What are we trying to accomplish?"

—39-year-old Business Unit President
Transaction and Information Processing Company

The Secret of Proactive Seduction

Never present something to a group before you've lobbied them individually.

▲

There is a Japanese concept that I think is totally applicable to American companies as well. It works very well for me.

It's called *nemoashi*.

It means respect for the individual and consensus building.

Before I go to a meeting to discuss a controversial issue—for example, if I know that I'm going to need your support to do this—I'm going to talk to you ahead of time.

We'll sort out where we disagree, versus having a big confrontation. The thought of having a knock-down, drag-out, American-style debate in public is just not something you'd ever do with the Japanese.

To go to a meeting in Japan and bring up an issue with everyone else in the room—an important issue, a controversial one that you've never discussed with that individual before—is the absolute worst thing you can do. It shows no respect for that person. You didn't even deem them worthy to talk to ahead of time.

If I lobby you beforehand, at least I had the decency to sit down and talk to you about it ahead of time so you didn't come in and get blindsided, and if I win and you lose, that's okay, but at least it was done aboveboard.

This is probably useful in small companies, too.

▲
___

You have to be able to go outside your authority and get things done, and the only way you're going to do that is by having relationships with the people involved. *Nemoashi*. It all comes down to respect for the individual, in the sense that I'm going to take the time to explain an issue to you ahead of time.

▲
___

—38-year-old Senior Vice President, Sales and Marketing
Consumer Product Company

The Secret of Cooperative Inspiration

If you share ownership of your ideas with others, they can help your good ideas become great ones.

▲

I have really changed in the past three years. What I used to do was sit people down and say, "I want to do this. Let's do it."

Now I bring people in and say, "Hmm, we have this problem. What should we do about it?"

I will keep people here for a long time talking about it. We keep talking about it until somebody else comes up with the idea.

Then I will push it a little further. I might keep asking questions. Pretty soon they're going down the path. Somebody else is going down the path I wanted to go down.

▲

It may take three times as long, but all of a sudden they think I'm a much nicer person. I'm championing their idea. And I'm

not pushing my idea on them. It does take longer, but it's not as alienating. People can get ahead by bullying their way through. But it's rare, and I think it's also rare that it's sustained when they do. At some point, somebody gets them.

▲

You don't have to be liked all the time, and you do want to be respected more than liked. But I think it certainly doesn't hurt to not have a lot of enemies.

To the extent that you can bring other people in, give other people the opportunity to get on board at their own speed, you benefit.

You get a better result that way.

People will come up with maybe a slight variation that's actually better. Or someone brings up an idea, and somebody else brings up a counter-argument that's good and valid. And someone else figures out a tweak to make it right.

—37-year-old Senior Vice President
Financial Institution

The Secret of Synthetic Simplicity

The ability to analyze and simplify complexity is becoming a crucial career skill.

▲

▲

If there's one skill you really need today, it's to be capable of synthesis.

▲

My job is to try to synthesize out the vision and fundamental strategy for the company, in all sectors. It's kind of the ultimate challenge.

My responsibilities are to try to sort out how the total portfolio works.

Literally from my earliest days here, the top management of this company have sought me out to help them understand what really matters, what really makes sense, and to cut through a lot of the superfluous data that is clogging the system here.

Most people are incapable of what I would call "synthetic thought."

Synthesis. That's what's really required for leadership in any dimension of life.

There are many very, very well educated, very bright people who have either never been trained or understood the value of doing that type of thinking.

There's a type of thought that's linear, analytical, logical—A + B = C. That's what they teach in school, in business school, particularly.

There's another type of thought which is intuition, where you take in a lot of inputs and come up with something new, but it may not have all the elements that were involved in the inputs.

The third type of thought is synthesis, where you take in a lot of inputs and you put together a new construct. And you can find literally every piece of the inputs contained in the new construct.

We're constantly bombarded with information, with insights, with opinions, perspectives.

Analysts will make the world more complex. The analyst will turn out reams and reams of data—maybe some information but damned little synthesis. Rarely will they simplify the world for you. They'll probably make it more complex.

What you have to be capable of doing is taking all that in and synthesizing it into a construct that makes sense, where you can find those various pieces in the new construct.

If you're capable of that type of thought, you can make the world simple.

▲

What companies need more than anything else right now is people who can simplify things, not make them more complex.

▲

Make things simple enough so that your company can make decisions and move in a given direction.

—40-year-old Strategic Planning Executive
Automobile Manufacturer

Acknowledgments

We are most grateful to the sixty executives who took time out from very busy schedules to share their career insights with us. Their candor and enthusiasm for the project was remarkable.

The advice and encouragement given us by Nanscy Neiman, Maureen Egen, and Anne Hamilton of Warner Books was invaluable.

Joseph Hooper did a superb job helping to conduct the interviews, and Rebecca Reisman was a major help in the research stage.

Our agent, Mel Berger at William Morris, gave us expert assistance in putting the project together.

We thank everyone at the Time Warner Research Library, especially Mary Pradt, Anne Schmutz, Angela Thornton, and Karen McCree. The crew at A Steno Service in New York, especially Caroline Downing and Leticia Medina, did a heroic job transcribing the interviews.